Janell

Janell

by

Jerry B. Jenkins

MOODY PRESS
CHICAGO

To Mike and the real Janell

ISBN:0-8024-4322-2

1 2 3 4 5 6 7 Printing/LC/Year 88 87 86 85 84 83

Printed in the United States of America

Chapter One

Very few people who heard of the death of shipping magnate Adrian Rudolph on the news the morning of August 22 had any inkling that it was anything but an accident. Including me, but of course, neither did I have any reason to think I would care one way or another.

But I would.

Bonnie, our matronly receptionist, was arranging the boss's messages when he burst through the double doors in characteristic fashion. "Whadya got for me, Bon?" the fat detective muttered as he charged by, sweeping his phone messages off her desk with one hand.

"Good morning, Mr. Festschrift," she said to his back. "I have those for you."

"Congratulations, Wally," I said, hardly looking up as he lumbered by. His too-heavy-for-the-weather-but-I'm-too-hard-on-lightweight trousers sported a heavy damp circle over his right thigh, probably out of his vision.

"For what?" he said, slowing a bit and puffing from the journey from his apartment down the hall, not forty feet away. "And what're you workin' on anyway?"

"For what I read in the paper," I said, staring at

the damp circle on his pants. "And what I'm doing is hunting and pecking my way to the conclusion of my report on that inside shoplifting job at Suburban Grocery."

"Oh, yeah, I'll bet you're glad that plum assignment is over, huh, Spence?"

I nodded, realizing where Wally was getting the liquid on his pant leg. He never carried a handkerchief, so when the sweat accumulated on his forehead, as it would every two or three minutes on a scorcher like that morning, he just swiped at it with an open right palm and deposited it somewhere above his knee.

"You read about me in the paper, huh? Hey, where's your wife?"

I couldn't keep up with Wally's ability to switch subjects in mid-stream. As I sat there at the typewriter trying to decide which question to answer first, Bonnie rescued me. "Margo is out on the school vandalism case, and yes, of course, we all read about you in the paper. Have you seen it?"

"I heard it on the radio, but I haven't seen it yet, no. You got one around here?"

Bonnie and I each produced our copies. He accepted both. "Hey, I'm going to want that back, Wally," Bonnie said.

"Me too," I said.

"Yeah, yeah," he said, stuffing his phone messages in his pocket and leaning over my desk to spread out the front page. Under the headline "Festschrift Charges Dropped; To Receive Full Pay," Wally read:

"Charges that former Chicago Homicide Detective Sergeant Walvoord F. Festschrift, 59, violated police department rules last year were dropped today in the wake of heavy public sentiment.

"The veteran investigator, an expert in forensics who had served for more than thirty years on the Chicago force—the last nineteen as a homicide sergeant—had been suspended pending investigation of his releasing classified information and moonlighting as a consultant to a private detective agency without permission from his superiors.

"The case stemmed from the murder of U.S. Postal worker Lloyd Cavenaugh, 53, which was believed to have been committed by Timothy Bemis, a Vietnam war veteran who claimed to have been missing in action in southeast Asia at the time of the crime.

"Chicago Police closed the investigation, but Bemis's younger sister, Lindsey, 25, sought the help of the Glencoe-based EH Detective Agency, owned by Earl Haymeyer, now head of the Illinois Department of Law Enforcement.

"Sergeant Festschrift, who was not involved in the initial investigation and had made no secret of his contention that it had been mishandled by Chicago police, reportedly provided photos and documents to Miss Bemis, who in turn made them available to EH Detective Agency personnel.

"When Festschrift was suspended for the alleged misconduct, he went to work for the EH Agency, which he now heads in Haymeyer's absence. The agency, with the help of Festschrift, turned up the real killer, Texas-born Raymond A. Harris of New Mexico. Bemis was freed and public sentiment in the Festschrift case turned toward the suspended sergeant.

"The city's decision to dismiss the charges will result in back pay of more than fifty thousand dollars to Festschrift and early retirement with full pay until age sixty-five, when he will receive his standard pension.

"Lawyers for Festschrift say he will continue as head of . . ."

As if he hadn't read what Margo and I had read at breakfast and Bonnie had read upon arriving for work, Wally looked up sheepishly and said, "So it was an inside job at Suburban Grocery, huh, Philip?"

I nodded, knowing he didn't really want any details just then. He could read them in my report. "Wally," I said, "we're really pleased for you. All of us."

"Yeah? Well, hey, me too, ya know?" he said, laughing and embarrassed. He shuffled into his office and closed the door. In less than a minute he was out again. "So who's Adrian Rudolph?" He was peering at one of the tiny slips of paper containing his phone messages.

"You didn't get a call from him," I said. "He's dead."

"I know," Wally said, eyes still on the message. "This gal leaves a message that she wants to talk to me about his death. Who is he?"

"Head of some big conglomerate is all I know," I said. "Lived at Lake Point Towers, worked in the city."

"What conglomerate?"

I shrugged.

"Bonnie!" Wally hollered. "You got any idea who this, ah, Rudolph worked for?"

"Yes, sir, I believe he was head of Mid-America something."

"You mean Mid-America Maritime?"

"That's it, yes."

"And he died recently?"

4

"Right," I said. "Margo and I heard it on the news this morning. Electrocuted himself trying to water his lawn." I almost smiled, it sounded so weird, but I had long since learned not to joke with Wally Festschrift about anyone's death. He had a sense of humor, of course, but I guess he'd seen too much death in his lifetime to see any humor in that.

"Thought you said he lived at Lake Point," Wally said.

"This was at his summer cottage in Wisconsin."

"Head of a big conglom like that waters his own lawn?"

"I don't know, Wally. I can't imagine a rich guy like that taking servants to his cottage, can you?"

"You bet I can. If he's really head of Mid-America Maritime, he's gotta be makin' about a million dollars a year. I'll bet he was chauffeur-driven to his lake!"

"So who wants to talk to you about his death?" I asked.

"Ah, lemme see here, Janell Barnard."

I flinched when he said Janell. The only Janell I had ever known was Janell Springmont, my first and only true love at Ohio State. Of course, until I met Margo I didn't know what real love was, but I had cared more for Janell than anyone I'd ever gone with before, and giving her up was one of the most painful decisions of my life.

"Not *Bar*nard," Bonnie piped up. "Bar*nard*. She made that very clear."

"Well, excuse me," Wally mocked. "What else did Miss Bar*nard* say? She think he was murdered? And who is she anyway?"

Bonnie flashed a resigned smile. "To answer your

5

questions in order: not much, she didn't say, and she was his administrative assistant. Also, she's not a *Miss*. She's a *Mrs.*"

"That important?"

"She seemed to think so, Wally," Bonnie said. "Why not call her?"

"Ah, I don't have time," he said, leaving his doorway and handing the message back to Bonnie. "Just give her an appointment for tomorrow morning after our staff meeting, 'bout nine-thirty I guess. And see if she'll say any more about what she wants to talk about. A secretary sometimes knows more'n anyone else about a dead guy."

"That's another thing she's a bit sensitive about, Wally," Bonnie said.

"What now?"

"She was not his secretary; she was his administrative assistant."

"Well, la-dee-da."

It was all I could do to finish my case report and drop it in Wally's basket. Just hearing the name Janell had stricken me with memories. I'd met Janell Springmont when I was a sophomore art student in Columbus, and she was a freshman in business. We dated steadily for three years.

"You want another case, cowboy, or are you gonna take the rest of the day off?" Wally chided as I left his office without even a grunt.

"Oh, yeah, sure, Wally. I'm free."

"I was just teasing, Philip, because I *do* want you to take the rest of the day off. I've got some interesting cases we can talk about at tomorrow morning's meeting. Why don't you go home and surprise your wife

6

by having dinner ready for her when she gets there?
I'll see if I can coax her out of here a little early today,
too."

"Are you sure, Wally? Isn't there anything I can
do?"

He reached into a bulging file cabinet behind him.
"Sure. You can read up on this case, but don't do
anything until we've talked about it. We may not
even take it, you know."

I went back to my desk and started leafing through
the file, but I was reading without seeing. Memories
had taken over my mind.

"Philip!" Wally shouted, making me jump. "I
meant for you to take it *home* and read it. What'sa
matter, you not gonna take my advice and fix your
wife's dinner tonight?"

"Wally, we share the housework, but I can't cook!"

"Then take her out, but get outa here! You deserve
a break, so take it!"

"I've got nothing planned."

He swore. "Then go home and do nothing!"

I drove to our Winnetka apartment thinking about
Janell and wracking my brain to remember what I
had and hadn't told Margo about her. By the time
Margo arrived home around three o'clock, I had
worked myself into a frenzy. I tried to act casual.

Somehow Margo had the ability to look cool and
fresh when the rest of the world was sweating. I had
the air conditioner going full blast and was still miser-
able. She came in and kicked her shoes off as she
hugged me. Her naturally dark complexion was lumi-
nescent from the sun, and in a cream, sleeveless dress

7

she was cool to the touch. I wondered how long we'd be married before I'd lose the thrill of holding her.

"I'm glad you're my wife," I said.

She smiled. "What's with Wally today?" she said. "He need some time alone or something?"

I wasn't listening. "I'm taking you out to dinner tonight," I said.

"I gathered that from Wally."

"Where do you want to go?"

"Anywhere cool."

"We have to talk, Margo."

"We do?"

"Yeah, you know about that guy who was electrocuted in Wisconsin, the executive from Chicago?"

"Yeah, the big shot. Wally told me he heard from somebody in the company today, but he has no idea what she wants yet. She's coming in in the morning." Margo eyed me warily. "What do we need to talk about, Philip?"

I hesitated, wondering if I'd regret dredging it up. "Janell," I said finally.

"Janell? Your old flame? Are you sure I want to hear this? Remember I have no old boyfriends to tell you about."

"I know," I said, scowling.

"Didn't you already tell me about her?"

"Yeah, mostly I guess."

"But there's something more?"

"I don't know. I just feel like I need to tell you, to get it off my chest."

Margo's smile faded, and she slowly walked away from me. "Um, Philip, what has this got to do with the big shot who was killed?"

"Oh, nothing. It's just that Janell was the name of the girl, the, uh, woman who called Wally about it. It just brought her to mind, I guess."

"But that Janell isn't your Janell, is it?"

"No. At least I don't think so. She could have married. Probably did. But it would be a wild coincidence."

"Uh-huh," she said, turning back toward me and looking me in the eye. "But anyway, it brought your Janell to mind and—"

"C'mon, Margo, don't call her 'my Janell.' This is hard enough as it is."

"I didn't mean anything by it, Philip. But she was yours for a time, wasn't she?" I shrugged and nodded. "And you two were very close for a few years."

"Right."

"If there's anything more to tell me than that, sweetheart, I'm not sure I want to hear it. I should say, I'm quite sure I *don't* want to hear it."

She turned away from me again, and I wasn't sure what to say.

"I could have taken it if you had given it to me all at once when you first told me about the previous women in your life," she said quietly. "But once I'd been filled in and you told me that you never really loved anyone until me, I assumed that was all there was to it."

"That *is* all there was to it!" I said, a little too loudly. "I mean, I'm not saying there was anything there that I regret or that we shouldn't have done or anything. It's just that I maybe tried to gloss over it a bit too quickly the first time I mentioned her, and sometimes that makes me feel guilty."

9

"Why?"

"Because I don't want to even think about her and that time and how painful it was. What it did to me, and to her."

"I guess you'd better tell me about it, Philip. And then, can we be done with it? I can't say dealing with other women is one of my strengths yet, even if they *are* from the distant past."

Chapter Two

We agreed to save the discussion for dinner at The Indian Trails, about a six-block walk, and we took advantage of Wally's generosity by whiling away the heat of the late afternoon at the apartment house pool.

At about six we walked in silence, holding hands, to the restaurant. We loved each other with our eyes as we waited in line to be seated. After we had ordered, Margo looked at me expectantly, as if she had endured the tension long enough.

"I'm already tired of sharing your mind with this girl, Philip," she said. "Let's get it out and put it behind us, OK?"

I nodded. "It's just that I guess I never really told you that this girl was special."

Margo seemed a bit annoyed. She looked away quickly and ran a hand through her long, dark hair. "All your girls are special. Me you married. Allyson you *could have* married. Could you have married this girl too?"

"Probably, yes."

"Wonderful. Are you beginning to wonder if you did the right thing in marrying me?"

"Don't do that, Margo. You know better than that." She didn't respond. "I just want to tell you a

11

little more about how it ended; that's all. Or how it almost didn't end." That caused a double-take, and I knew she was wondering how recently I might have seen Janell Springmont.

"I haven't seen her for more than seven years," I said, mostly to put Margo's mind at ease. "And I hardly ever think of her. But I have to admit that when I see someone who looks like her, or when I hear her name—which I hadn't until today—it brings back painful memories."

"I thought this was the girl *you* broke up with, not the other way around."

"It was. That's just it. It still wasn't easy. You·get used to someone after three years. We were comfortable together. We didn't squabble. We had plans. Nothing official, but we were an item among our friends."

"So why did you break it off, if it was going to be so painful? And why didn't you get back together, besides the fact that it wasn't meant to be and God intended you for me?"

She was smiling slightly, and that encouraged me.

I reached across the table to hold her hand. "I believe that," I said, "though, of course, I didn't know it at the time. My mother always said that God wants to replace good with better and better with best and best with His perfect will. You're His perfect will, Margo."

She smiled, but said, "If God replaces your idea of best with His perfect will, that makes her best."

"You shoulda been a lawyer. Let me remind you that you replaced anybody and everybody in my life. You're so far out in front of everyone else I ever thought I cared for—and there haven't been many—that I never even think to compare them with you. I just wanted to be sure you knew where my head was on Janell, because I want to be able to quit thinking about her."

"Me too. You think you'll quit thinking about her once I know the whole story?"

"I hope so. You see, until I met you, I thought Janell Springmont was the loveliest creature I'd ever seen."

"You didn't change your mind when you met me, Philip. I was a sniveling, suicidal weakling."

"Granted. But when you came around, your beauty was obvious."

"This is the way I like to argue."

"And the girl you like to discuss," I said.

"Guilty. Anything wrong with wanting my husband to want to think and talk about me?"

"Hardly."

"Then get done with what's-her-name, willya?"

"Well, I never thought Janell was committed to her faith; that's all. She was thin and lithe and beautiful in a soft sort of way. We got along, like I said, but for three years she seemed silent about my faith, let alone hers. She wanted me to pray, but she never did. We went to Christian activities on campus, but she was always on the fringe. I would press her about it, but that's not easy to do with someone you think you're in love with.

"I didn't want to offend her, and when it came right down to it, I realized I didn't want to lose her. I liked being seen with her—I admit it. She was my life, and we had fun, but I came to realize that while she

13

said she had received Christ and went to church—
because she always had—that was the extent of it.
And she wasn't really open to my advice about it."

"Which was?"

"Just that she ought to get serious about it. Make
Christ part of her life, not just something for Sundays
or 'religious' times. A big thing among the Christians
on campus during those years was the idea that all of
life pertained to God; you couldn't pigeonhole Him
into one corner and pretend He didn't apply to the
secular world."

"But she fought that?"

"That's just it—I wish she had. We rarely argued,
and never about that. She would just tell me she
agreed, but I knew when I was pushing, and I didn't
want to come off like a spiritual big brother or holier-
than-thou."

"Which was a danger," Margo agreed. "There's
nothing more obnoxious than someone who thinks
he's everyone's pastor."

"Unless he is."

She nodded.

"So, anyway, the time came, about midway
through my senior year, when I started thinking seri-
ously about my future. I wanted to go to art school,
maybe get married, settle down, all that. And I realized that whenever I thought about that, I didn't
imagine Janell in the picture with me. The wife I
daydreamed about when I imagined my future was a
nameless, faceless woman, someone I hadn't met
yet."

"How did we get to talking about me all of a sudden?" she asked with a smile.

"I don't know," I admitted. "I never really put that together until now. You know, I *was* thinking about you, even loving you, planning for you, longing for you, before I ever knew you."

Margo was beginning to enjoy the conversation. "And you were the man of my dreams," she said with a mischievous sparkle, "though you weren't nameless and faceless."

"I wasn't? You knew what I'd look like?"

"I thought I did. I used Clark Gable's Rhett Butler as the substitute vision until I met you."

"What a disappointment I must have been! I can't even grow a moustache. Otherwise, Clark and I could be twins, couldn't we?"

"Identical."

We didn't talk much as we ate, but we walked home the long way. No coolness came with the twilight, but the razor-sharp bite of the sun was gone. We sat on a bench in the park. "I just gradually realized that I had lost interest in Janell."

"Lost interest? Just like that?"

"Well, it was a long process. But the spark was gone. I didn't have that thrill of anticipation when I was going to see her. I felt guilty when I was with her, because I was going through the motions, but I didn't love her anymore."

"Could she tell?"

"I thought so. She seemed to become much more interested in me. She worked harder at pleasing me, at being what she thought I wanted her to be."

"Even as a Christian?"

"No. Just as a girl friend. But that was awkward for me. I had always enjoyed the idea that I was dating someone I thought was too good for me; you know, the type that makes people say, 'Wow, how did he land *her?*' "

"How well I know."

"Oh, come on, Margo. People react that way when they see us, but it's because of you, and you know it."

"I do not!"

"Well, good. We each think the other is too good for us. That's the way it should be, I guess. Anyway, except for the fact that she never got serious about her faith, I felt she was ahead of me in every way. She was bright, beautiful, popular. I enjoyed wondering what she saw in me and knowing other people were wondering the same thing. It was an ego trip to be seen with her."

"That's a high compliment for a woman."

"I feel the same about you, only more so."

"And I find that hard to believe."

"That's what makes you so special, Margo."

"Did Janell Springmont know how you felt?"

"Sure, but when I started to lose interest and she sensed it, she started acting as if she felt the same about me."

"I'm not following you."

"Well, it's just that when I felt like the luckiest one, I enjoyed the relationship, but when she started acting like it was a privilege to be going with me, it made things worse. I had lost interest, and now I felt strange that she was trying to hang on."

"What did you do?"

"I didn't want to be mean. I mean, I didn't want to just drop a bomb on her after three years, so I started

16

becoming less available, more interested in other things."

"Don't tell me, let me guess," Margo said. "It didn't work, and you would have been better off to just tell her."

"Right. I had to become more and more obvious, and finally she got the message. Then she demanded that I just say it, just tell her what the problem was."

"And did you?"

"I tried not to. I was young and inexperienced. I had never told a woman I had supposedly adored and felt unworthy of that I had changed my mind and was no longer interested. I'd been on the receiving end of that a time or two, and I knew the pain."

"How did you tell her?"

"I started by just answering her questions. She asked, 'Are you trying to tell me something? Have I done something wrong? Don't you love me anymore? Do you know I still love you and probably more than ever? Is there something I can do, something I can change, something I can stop doing to make you love me again?'"

"That must have hurt."

"You can't imagine."

"Yes, I can. It's what I would ask if you ever fell out of love with me, Philip."

"Margo, our love is different. That wasn't love. It was infatuation, puppy love, whatever you want to call it. I love you not because I can't help it, though I can't. I also choose to love you, so even when we get used to each other and the big-time tingles go away, I'll still love you. I'll always love you. I promised I would, and I will."

17

"But you couldn't say that to Janell."

"No. I couldn't."

"How did you answer her?"

"Honestly."

"Really? You told her it was because she wasn't serious enough about her faith?"

"Yes."

"And what did you say when she asked what she could do to keep you?"

"I told her there was nothing she could do. And I told her that it must have been something deeper than just a change of attitude on her part. Because something had caused me to lose my feelings for her, and while I would always care for her and remember her and the good times we had, I didn't foresee being in love with her again, no matter what."

"Ouch."

"Yeah, I know. But Margo, you know, I got some advice from a sisterly-type friend back then. Name was Melinda. Good Christian kid. Married a friend of mine. Anyway, she was advising me at the time, and she said, 'Painful as it is for both of you, Philip, you've got to tell her. Shut the door and leave it shut unless you *know* things will change.' She convinced me it would be worse if I left some ray of hope there for Janell, especially when there was none."

"You mean, even if she had changed and become a vibrant Christian, it was over for you two?"

"That's right, and that's just it, Margo. She *did* change. She did become a vibrant Christian."

"Just for you?"

"I didn't know. I hoped not. I told her that I wanted to see her get closer to Christ, but that that was now totally divorced from our relationship. It may have had something to do with my loss of interest at first, but it wasn't the type of thing that would bring us back together. How could I know if it was just for me?"

"By how long her enthusiasm lasted after she saw that it wasn't going to do any good."

"And that I don't know."

"And that's what's bothering you now?"

"No. I don't know. I guess. Curiosity, you know. When we graduated she was active in church and a campus ministry, and she was still trying to keep in touch with me. She'd invite me to things, and sometimes I'd even go, to show her I was still her friend. But it became obvious that she wanted us back together, and while I was thrilled with her new enthusiasm for spiritual things, I couldn't pretend to still be interested in her romantically."

"But if you'd been convinced she was sincere?"

"I don't think so."

"How long did she keep pursuing you?"

"Through art school and while I was working in Atlanta."

"You mean even after we met?"

I nodded. "Let's just say that when I moved up here, I didn't leave a forwarding address."

"Is that it?"

"You mean, is that the whole story of Janell?"

"Uh-huh."

"Yeah."

"Just one question, Philip. If you knew beyond a doubt that Janell Springmont was solid and sincere, would it make you wish you hadn't dropped her?"

19

"No. She wasn't right for me. Somehow I knew that. I have to admit I'm very curious about her now, though, Margo. That's what I wanted to tell you."

She leaned forward and rested her chin on her fist. "Why don't you look her up?" she said.

"Look her up? Why? And where?"

"Just to satisfy your curiosity. Find out if she's married, who she married, if she has kids, where she works, what kind of memories she has. Unless you're afraid it'll stir some old passions. Then I wouldn't want you to do it."

"You want me to tell her I'm married and how happy I am."

"Top priority."

"You sure you wouldn't mind?"

"Not in the least. I trust you. I know you. I believe you. And I want her out of your system."

Chapter Three

When Bonnie asked if she could speak to me for a moment in the office the next morning, I begged off until after Wally's staff meeting. I wish now I hadn't.

The staff meetings, in our new, abbreviated agency, consisted of just Wally and Margo and me. Still, I didn't want to be late. They remained the highlight of our week. I remembered the good old days when Earl Haymeyer would invite Wally in as an expert. Larry Shipman was still with us, and so the four of us would sit under Wally's counsel and wind up more professional for it.

Now there were only two of us, but Wally was just as incisive and entertaining. Except that today he seemed to have little to talk about.

"We've got this secretary, ah, I mean administrative assistant, who worked for the guy with the reindeer name, ah, here it is, Adrian Rudolph. Her name's Bar*nard*, emphasis on the *nard*, please, and she wants to talk to me about Rudolph's death, so who knows? Apparently she thinks it's a suspicious death, or she wouldn't want to talk to me, right? If there's anything to it, I don't see anything else here that couldn't wait. Do you, Philip?"

"Sir?"

"Do you see anything pending here that can't wait if we need to move on this Rudolph death?"

"Uh, no, I guess not. I've only seen the one folder you gave me yesterday."

"Why don't we start then with you telling us the particulars?"

"Well, to tell you the truth I didn't really get a chance to study it yet, Wally."

"So you *did* take the day off yesterday, like I told you to! Good! Boy, I never have to worry about obedience to a directive like that, do I?"

"I'm sorry I didn't get to the case, Wally."

"Hey, think nothing of it. I'm serious. I was afraid you would spend the whole day poring over it and maybe have it solved by now. Lemme just run it down for you two. You got it handy?"

"Sure, jes' a minute," I said, feeling like a fool for having left the case folder on my desk. What did I think the meeting was all about, anyway?

I jogged out to my desk, snatched the file, and was just whirling around to head back into Wally's office when I saw her. In the rattan chair next to Bonnie's desk, staring expressionless at me, was Janell Springmont. She raised her head only slightly and appeared as if she was about to speak, but I just kept moving and turned away as if I had never seen her.

But I had. And I knew then that that must have been what Bonnie wanted to tell me. That Janell had mentioned my name. That she had somehow discovered where I worked, and when she needed the help of private detectives, she knew where to come. The question now was, did she really need help, or was she still chasing me?

I had no illusions about my appeal. I'm an average guy who never had a lot of girl friends. Never more than one at a time, that's for sure. But I had rejected her, and maybe that was something she couldn't live with. I didn't know. All I knew was that Janell Barnard and Janell Springmont were one and the same, and I was speechless, and breathless.

I was glad for the chance to sit in silence as Wally intoned from the file all the information about a suspected embezzlement from a suburban shopping mall. "They don't want the police in on it," he said. "Makes sense. Problem is, none of us are that good with financial records, are we?"

Margo shook her head. I wasn't listening.

"Philip?" Wally queried again.

"Yes?" I said, huffing and puffing as if I'd just run a mile. Margo stared at me, wondering why the trot to my desk had had such an effect on me.

"You good with financial records?" Wally asked. "Could you spot an embezzlement if you had enough time with the books?"

"Oh, uh, no sir. No, I couldn't, I don't think. No."

I was still sucking air and realized that I had held my breath from the minute I had seen Janell to the time Wally had asked the question. The years had been good to her. Her hair was longer and her face was still youthful, though she didn't have that babylike softness of a twenty-two-year-old anymore.

"Well, we'd have to bring in an expert then," Wally said. "I know a few, but they're expensive. We might do better to get a bright student to help us."

We both nodded, but Wally quickly tired of that

23

case and dug out another. It was a domestic problem. "I thought we didn't take those," Margo said.

"We don't, but this one is interesting," Wally said. "The mistress wants us to follow the guy to see if he still acts affectionate to his wife, because if he does, she'll bow out of the picture. I love it!"

Margo pursed her lips and shook her head. "Welcome to the new age," she said. "Maybe we should just take the case for a day, tell the mistress he's blissfully in love with his wife, and save a marriage."

"Problem is, that ain't gonna save the marriage, and we all know it," Wally said. "So can I assume there's consensus here that we won't be takin' this case?" We nodded. He added, "An' I think we're gonna take our ad out of the Yellow Pages. People lookin' for what we do ain't readin' the phone book."

Wally stood and replaced the two folders in his credenza, grabbed another half dozen and settled in again. "OK, I think I told you both yesterday that there were some interesting things coming up today. We'll hold on the shopping mall embezzlement until I can locate a numbers man, and I'll call the jealous mistress and tell her to try Quick Harry's Private Detection and Night Watch Company. Meanwhile, we've got plenty to keep us busy right here."

He patted the pile of thick folders and looked back and forth between us as if begging the question. I was still having trouble breathing, let alone speaking.

"I'll bite," Margo said finally. "What've you got?"

"Something that had to wait until today; that's a clue."

"Oh, goodie," Margo said, "just what we need. A mystery."

"C'mon, girl," Wally said, feigning a wound. "Don't you wanna play?"

"Sure, but that's not enough of a clue this early in the morning. Tell us more."

"Why would certain cases have to wait until today?" he said. "Why would I have something I can work on now that I couldn't have worked on, now listen, *before* yesterday?"

Margo shifted into hyper-thought, and I was tempted to tell Wally to get on with it because his next appointment was here. Another part of me wanted to put it off as long as possible. I was glad I hadn't tried to tell Margo that Janell was less than beautiful. But what did she want?

"So it has something to do with your exoneration by the City?"

Wally nodded.

"Police department cases?"

He nodded again.

"Unsolved murder cases?"

He smiled.

"How will we be paid?" Margo asked. "Unsolved murder cases are open to almost anyone who wants to volunteer for a little practice."

"Who would pay to have murder cases solved, given that the City wouldn't?" he said. "I mean, who would both pay and give us all the background information?"

"I.D.L.E.," I said.

"Right! The Illinois Department of Law Enforcement. Earl would like to see some of these cases

25

solved so he can put the spotlight on the Chicago P.D. and make some changes there. He gave the stuff to me months ago, but he couldn't turn me loose on it until this thing with the City was cleared up. He's not at all happy with their homicide investigation record."

"Especially now that you're gone?" Margo tried.

"Hey, today ain't payday, honey," Wally said, laughing. "Save the strokes till Friday."

"Any good ones?" I asked.

"Yeah, a few. I was thinkin' maybe we'd each take one and handle it in our down time. Any time anybody gets onto something hot or interesting, the other two of us drop what we're doing and pitch in."

"Sounds like fun," Margo said. "Anyway, maybe it's just my imagination, but it seems to me business is a little slack."

"It *is*," Wally said. "Let's face it, hiring private detectives is a luxury not too many can afford. Blame it on the economy." He looked at his watch. "Hey, I've got an appointment. Listen, here, why don't each of you take three of these and read them through? Then trade, and we'll talk about 'em in a week and start divvyin' 'em up. Fair enough?"

As we walked toward the door with our files under our arms, Margo said something light, and Wally laughed. She looked at me, but I hadn't even heard her. I was holding my breath again and hoping to hide behind her in case we passed Janell on her way in. Margo could tell I was upset, but there was no time to ask me about it.

Margo opened the door, and I nearly ran her over

trying to stay close behind. "Well, Philip!" she said when I didn't even excuse myself.

"I'm sorry, Mar," I said, "uh, listen, let me see your cases, huh?"

She looked puzzled, but I was so intent on looking busy when we came out that I reached for her file folders and dropped my own. I had visions of Janell appearing above me, so I just scooped them up, getting the material from three different cases all mixed in together."

"I've gotta call that guy, you know, from Suburban Grocery," I said, nearly shouting as the air I had been holding in burst forth. "I'll talk to you later."

Margo furrowed her brow and went to her desk, then smiled and nodded to the girl in the rattan chair.

"OK, Bon!" Wally yelled from his office.

Bonnie flashed an apologetic look at Janell, as if to say she'd been trying to train the man to use the intercom. She leaned over and spoke into hers. "She's on her way, sir." But Wally didn't even have his turned on.

"You say somethin'?" he hollered.

"She's on her way, Wally!" Bonnie said as sweetly as possible at that volume.

By now Margo was reading her first case, but I couldn't resist a quick peek as Janell stood. She had that casual look of the very wealthy, as if she was unaware of her ultra-expensive clothes. I shouldn't have looked.

She headed straight for my desk and stopped in front of me, smiling down at me with a look that transcended the years.

I couldn't speak.

"Philip," she said.

I stood and opened my mouth, but nothing came out. I cleared my throat and tried again. "Hi, Janell," I managed. By now Margo was looking, and I was crimson.

"What kind of a greeting is that for an old friend?" she said. And with Margo watching and Wally in the doorway to see where his appointment was, Janell moved around to the side of my desk and wrapped her arms around my neck.

I dropped my hands to my sides so they wouldn't be between us, and as she embraced me and whispered in my ear how lovely it was to see me again and how was I and all that, I was looking right at Margo—who enjoyed seeing me in the predicament.

"I've been fine, Janell, and I'd like you to meet—" but she stopped me with a glossy kiss right on the mouth! I almost jerked away, but I didn't want to embarrass her. I certainly didn't return the kiss, but stared wide-eyed over Janell's shoulder at Margo, who threw her head back and covered her mouth to keep from bursting into laughter.

"My wife!" I shouted as Janell pulled back, and I pointed at Margo, who stood.

"Oh, my!" Janell exulted. "Your wife! And isn't she darling? Hi! I'm Janell Springmont Bar*nard*, emphasis on the *nard*."

"Hi, Mrs. Bar*nard*," Margo said, unable to resist emphasizing the last syllable a little more than necessary. "I've heard a lot about you. I'm Margo Franklin Spence, emphasis on the Spence." And she smiled.

Janell took Margo's hands in hers and turned to

28

look at me as I wiped her pale gloss from my lips with the back of my hand. "How cute she is, Philip! Just darling!" she said, as if talking about a dog. "You're a lucky man."

"I know," I muttered.

"And you, young lady, you're a lucky girl!"

"I know," Margo repeated with a huge grin. "And don't you forget it."

"Oh, and she's quick, too! I like that, Philip! You've got yourself a real winner here! And possessive!"

Wally stepped from his doorway. "I take it you two know each other?" he said. "Or is that restating the obvious?" He raised his eyebrows at me.

"We went to college together," I said miserably, stealing a glance at a still beaming Margo. Later I would be proud of her when I remembered this moment, but now all I wanted to do was sit down.

"Oh, we did more than that together, Philip!" Janell said, winking at Margo.

"Won't you come in, Mrs. Barnard?" Wally said, guiding her by the elbow and then shutting the door.

Margo smiled mischievously at me and turned back to her reading, but Bonnie approached. "She said she knew you from college, Philip," she said. "But really!"

"We used to go together," I said quietly.

"Well, I gathered *that*, for Pete's sake!" Bonnie said. She turned back to her desk. "I gathered that all right."

Margo was chuckling softly.

"Don't sit there with your back to me," I said.

"Oh, Philip!" she said, turning around and smiling

29

at me. "Aren't I a sweet, darling, possessive little thing?"

I shook my head, wishing I could hide.

"You didn't exactly tell me what type she was, Philip."

"I don't remember her being quite like that," I said.

After about half an hour of trying to rearrange the documents from the cases Wally had given me, I was startled by the sound of his door opening.

"Philip," he said, "could you join me for a little while?"

"Sure," I said, looking at Margo.

"You too, Margo," he said.

Chapter Four

What thirty minutes had done to Janell! It was hard to believe it was the same girl.

"I'm sorry," she kept saying through her tears. "It's just difficult. I'm sorry. You know better than anyone that this isn't like me, Philip. I'm sorry."

"It's been a long time, Janell, but you did seem fine a little while ago."

"Seeing you made me forget all my troubles, as usual," she said, trying to smile.

Here we go again, I thought.

"Well," I said, "I wouldn't exactly say you were your old self out there, either."

"It's the dope," she said, causing six raised eyebrows. "Oh, they're all legal! It's just that I've been in shock since Rudy's, since Mr. Rudolph's murder. The doctor gave me something to help me sleep and something to keep me going during the day. I'm sorry."

Suddenly she burst into laughter, making even Wally jump. "I didn't mean to say that about being in shock, while we're talking about Rudy electrocuting himself! Oh, that's not funny! What's wrong with me?" And then she was crying again, and apologizing.

"Uh, listen, Mrs. Barnard," Wally said, "why don't you let me fill in Philip and Margo here about what we've discussed so far, all right?"

She nodded, crying into a little hankie.

"Mrs. Barnard feels that her boss, Mr. Rudolph, Adrian Rudolph—ah, Philip, would you mind takin' a few notes here?—died in a suspicious manner. She's saying that certain people had cause to benefit from his death, and there may have been other motives as well. Is that right, Mrs. Barnard?"

She nodded and insisted that he call her Janell, which was probably more because he couldn't get the pronunciation correct than because she was ready to be informal with us.

"As long as we're getting this down, Janell," I said, "what is, or was, your boss's title?"

"President and chief executive officer, Mid-America Maritime Properties Corporation. His wife's name is Deirdre Rudolph, and they have three grown children, two daughters."

"Do I need all that?" I asked Wally.

"You need the wife's name. Let's wait and see if the kids fit in."

"That's right," Janell said, gaining control of herself. "You need the wife. Boy, do you need the wife. There's no remorse there, Philip, and—"

"All right, Janell," Wally said, "let's get the whole picture first before we get more specific, OK? Now, there's a corporation counsel—what was his name?"

"Fred Towns, Manfred S. Towns. And he's already seeing Mrs. Rudolph. Of course, they've been seeing each other right along, but he's been with her every minute since Rudy was killed, and he's using the excuse that he's an old friend of the family. Can you believe that?"

I was scribbling furiously.

"OK, Janell," Wally said gently. "Tell them about, ah, who's the other lawyer?"

"Zachary Hayes. Now he's nice, and so is his wife, Theresa. My former husband and I were friends with them."

"Former?" I asked.

"Yes, Bernard and I are divorced. No children, luckily."

Margo flinched.

"Your husband's name is Bernard Barnard?" I asked, incredulous.

"My *former* husband, yes. Don't think I didn't encourage him to use his middle name."

"Which was?"

"Chick. Who knows why?"

"Who knows why Bernard when his last name is Barnard? His parents must have hated him."

"His parents happen to be very well placed," she said.

"Not well placed enough to give the poor kid a decent name," Margo said. "I'm not sure Chick Barnard is any better, though, Janell, if you don't mind my saying so. Could easily grow into Chicken Barnyard, couldn't it?"

Janell ignored the remark. "I called him Beebee," she said, "because those were his initials."

"Now, tell me again how this Hayes character fits into the story."

"Well, he was Mr. Rudolph's personal lawyer, and he was about to draw up a will including the kids back into the estate, but—"

"Slow down a minute," Wally said, holding up an open palm. "Rudolph had a corporate lawyer who

33

was seeing his wife, and he had a private lawyer who was trying to get the kids back into his will. Why?"

"Because Mrs. Rudolph wanted them out. So did Rudy, for a while, but Zack brought him to his senses."

"Zack?"

"Zachary Hayes, his lawyer."

"Why were the kids written out of the will in the first place?"

"Because they were all environmental activists and wouldn't have anything to do with the business, the ingrates. Both Rudy and his wife, when they were relatively happy, wanted the kids to become part of the business. But the kids went off to school and decided that capitalism and money and everything else they'd enjoyed all their lives was a bunch of baloney. So they joined demonstrations and signed petitions, the whole bit, against their own father's company. Rudy felt they would come around, which they have. But she wanted them out of the will, and talked him into it by threatening the only thing he feared. Divorce."

"So, anyway, they came around. They're all married now, all in lucrative businesses, all very well-to-do. They were on speaking terms with Rudy and could even joke about the past, but the old lady, Deirdre, hasn't spoken to them for years. She told Mr. Rudolph that if he put them back in the will, she would divorce him. But the last communication I passed on to him from Zack was that he was free to change his will without her knowledge or consent."

"And?"

"The problem was, he wanted to change the will in a way that would affect her. When he took the kids

34

out, she got most of the estate, including his job and controlling stock in the company. He wanted her out of it except for a small amount of cash, about a million, I believe."

"A paltry sum," I said.

"To him it was," Janell said without looking at me. "And control of the company would have gone to his son."

"Interesting," Margo said.

"There's more," Janell said. "There's something else interesting about the timing of his death. Today is the sixteenth day in a twenty-day waiting period before we take over a smaller company. Some insiders think someone in the victimized company murdered Rudy, but I think that's just too convenient, especially when Deirdre is showing no remorse and is already sending out policy memos."

"Whoa," Wally said. "We're havin' trouble keepin' everybody straight, and this is where I came in. Let's take it from the top and get some details. Margo, what's the first question you would ask?"

Margo was ready. "Start by describing your late boss," she said. "What did he look like and what kind of a man was he?"

Janell looked as if she might break down again. She pressed her lips tight and got a faraway look in her eyes. "Raw power," she said softly. "The man oozed it. He would have been fifty-six years old this Friday, the twenty-sixth—the day the takeover was supposed to take place—yet he could have passed for his early forties in anybody's book. Tall, trim, smooth, great head of salt and pepper hair, worked out everyday, that type of a guy. Too good to be true. Always prepared, photographic memory, articulate, at ease with anybody. Tough. Firm. Demanding. Unflinching."

She could have been describing Earl Haymeyer, except he *was* in his early forties.

"And you were his assistant?" I asked.

"Administrative aide," she said. "Not a clerical person by any means, though I never hesitated to do anything he asked of me. I worshiped the man."

"Did his wife know that?" Margo asked.

"It wasn't *that* kind of worshiping, Mrs. Spence, not the way I worshiped your husband, for instance, but his wife wouldn't have cared anyway. That marriage had been over for years."

"Did he have another woman?" Margo asked.

"Besides whom?"

"I meant besides his wife."

"He had me."

"You just said you didn't worship him in that way."

"I didn't, and we weren't involved, if that's what you're driving at. But the companionship I provided him was all he needed."

"In other words, he had other women you didn't know about."

"I would have known about them. He wasn't out of my sight much. It cost me my marriage."

"Your husband thought you were more than business associates?"

"Not at all. Beebee knew better than that. He just couldn't compete with the sheer time that was required of me."

"How did you feel about that?" I asked, suddenly terribly grateful we hadn't stayed together.

"I told you I worshiped Rudy. I didn't worship Beebee. He was no great loss, and he did OK by me. I mean, I wouldn't have to work."

I couldn't stop myself. "You've changed," I said.

"That's where you're wrong," she said, looking deep into my eyes. I had to look away. I didn't know if she meant that how she felt about me had never changed, or that she had always been this ruthless without letting it show.

"You say Rudolph's wife shows no remorse?" Wally asked.

"That's right. She called all the vice-presidents and told them to report to her office yesterday afternoon. I asked her if she wanted me there, because I figured she'd need an aide too, you know. Not that I necessarily would have stayed long, but I wanted to hear what she had to say and see how she felt about losing her husband." Janell's lips quivered, and she held the hankie up to her eyes.

"So did you go?" Margo asked.

Janell shook her head and choked on her words. "She said she wouldn't be needing me anymore. She said my check was in the personnel office. It shouldn't have surprised me, I guess. She never did like me. Well, she's going to see me at least one more time."

"Where?"

"At the funeral. She can't keep me away from there. I want to see the charade she pulls. Probably show up with a black veil, crying and everything. You can bet she'll be leaning all over Freddie for support."

"Freddie?"

"Manfred Towns, the corporate counsel. My boss

was dead not one day before she was in the chair behind his desk, Freddie right there fawning beside her."

"Mr. Towns is not married either, I take it," Margo said.

"Many times. Not currently."

Margo shook her head. "This is beginning to sound like a soap opera," she said.

"It gets worse," Janell said. "Believe me."

"Show them the documents you showed me, Janell," Wally said.

"Oh, yes," she said, pulling them from her bag. "This is my proof that Rudy was just a few days away from changing his will. I don't know how Deirdre found out about it, but I'm convinced she did. Maybe Rudy mentioned something to Towns. He trusted him more than he should have. I tried to tell him."

We looked at the draft of a new will, unsigned, predated for September first, and containing brief marginal notes from Adrian Rudolph, who initialed each entry. Many of his comments were simply, "Good!" or, "Yes!" or, "Right! Thanks!"

I was intrigued by a cover note from the attorney, which was dated July 15 and had apparently stayed with all the correspondence through each delivery of the drafts of the will. Its hand-written message said, "Mr. Rudolph, get me a piece of your P.L. takeover, and this one and anything you want is on the house for a year."

The scribbled response from Rudolph read: "Dream a little dream, Z! Would love to, but it's too late this time. Maybe the next one."

"What's that all about?" I asked.

"Oh, just a joke really. Zack was telling Rudy he'd love to have a piece of the legal action on the takeover we're involved in with PlasTechs Limited, but then, who wouldn't? There'll be several million dollars in fees to lawyers and holding companies. If Zack had gotten a fraction of that he could have served Rudy gratis for the rest of his career."

"What's this takeover business all about?" I asked. "Mid-America is merging with someone, buying them out, what?"

Janell looked at me, drew a deep breath, and let it out slowly. "Have you got a few hours?" she asked.

"I don't know," I said. "I guess that's up to Wally. We taking this case, chief?"

"We haven't gotten that far yet," Wally said. "But I'll tell you this. If we do take it, we're all gonna need a crash course in business takeovers, because I've got a feeling that real enemies can be developed in these deals."

"Oh, they *can*," Janell confirmed. "In fact, there is tremendous animosity in this one. Why—"

Wally stopped her again with a gesture. "Janell, I'm afraid I'm going to have to ask you to save that until after we decide if we can help you. And to make that decision, I have to have one simple thing from you. I need to know why you think your boss died in a manner other than the way the Wisconsin State Police believe. They say he was electrocuted due to an electrical problem in his basement that sent a charge through his body when he turned on the sprinkler system."

Janell sighed. "I don't know all the particulars," she said. "But I know he's been sprinkling that lawn up there for twenty years and never had a problem before. I just think the timing was too coincidental. Five days from the finalization of the merger and ten days before his new will would have left the company to his son and the money to his son and daughters.

"Somebody did a number on him, Mr. Festschrift. And I'll pay you to find out who it is."

Chapter Five

"You certainly will," Wally said. "Especially if that's all we have to go on. There are a lot of people involved in this, which means I'd need to put all my people on it."

He scribbled a figure on the back of one of his business cards and slid it across the desk to her. "That's for a week or less. However long it takes us to find out if there was foul play. It's payable half in advance, and if at any point we decide the death was accidental, you pay the other half and it's over for us."

Margo was in a position to see the figure; I wasn't. All I knew was, Janell didn't bat an eye. She pulled out her checkbook and quickly wrote a check to cover the first half. "How long might it take you to decide if it was murder?"

"Shouldn't be more than a week."

"And how long after that to tell me who did it?"

"I wouldn't even want to try to answer that one, honey."

"I have a proposition for you."

"Shoot."

"Prove to me it was murder before midnight Thursday, and I'll double your fee. Give me at least enough evidence to stop the merger."

41

"I thought you were *for* the merger."

"I was. But now all I want is revenge. I don't want Deirdre Rudolph increasing her empire."

"You know, any two-bit agency could invent you enough evidence to postpone the merger."

"I don't want that. I knew Philip was at this agency and that it would be straight. Anyway, I don't want the merger postponed. I want it stopped."

"It's a deal, but let me tell you this. We won't be inventing anything just to get the money. And we're gonna need a lot of information from you if we're gonna get moving on this thing tomorrow morning. You free for dinner tonight?"

She nodded.

"Margo? Philip?"

I looked to her.

"Wouldn't miss it," she said.

I agreed.

When Janell was gone and Margo and I were back at our desks, I got her attention. "Psst."

She turned around.

"Well?" I said.

"Lovely," she said.

"I didn't mean that! How much?"

"Oh. Fifteen."

"Fifteen *thousand*, and she's gonna double it?"

"Fifteen big ones, Philip, but I wouldn't count on it. We're talking two days."

Wally emerged from his office and slipped me a piece of paper. "Philip, plan on driving up to that cottage tomorrow, and if this guy's available, have him go with you. He's an electrician. Tell him there's a couple of hundred in it for him. He'll insist on five.

42

Give him four. This is gonna be a fun one, kids. We're not in it for the money, but the challenge'll keep me goin' around the clock. Margo, get us some appointments at PlasTechs Limited for tomorrow afternoon. You through with that school vandalism case?"

"Yes, but they should pay me as a psychologist rather than a detective."

"How so?"

"Well, you know you can never actually catch vandals. No one admits anything or brags about it. It's not even worth a badge of honor among your friends because it's such an act of cowardice. So I recommended that the school make public a post office box where the vandals could send money to pay for the damages. They also announced that anyone who wanted to donate, guilty or not, could feel free."

"That worked? I'm impressed but amazed."

"It didn't work at first. Then they announced that until every penny came in there would be no extracurricular events. None at all."

"That your idea too?"

"Yeah."

"How'd they do?"

"They made more than three hundred dollars *profit*."

Wally roared.

That night at Carrollton's in Evanston I was struck by the somber mood at our table compared to the gaiety all around us. This was hardly the place to discuss murder, but we were pressed for time.

Our client had found the time to have her hair done and was striking in a dark, long, semiformal summer gown. Margo and I sat across from each other at the square table with Wally to my left and Janell to my right. That proved to be a mistake. Every time she made a significant point, she grabbed my arm. I could feel the ice from Margo, but what could I do?

Over the kind of meal Wally loves—all the goodies from bread to crackers to appetizers to soup to salad and through the main courses to dessert—we quizzed Janell Barnard.

Wally honed in on the fact that apparently Rudolph was killed just before he was to have been picked up for the ride back to Chicago.

"That's right, Mr. Festschrift," Janell said. "He usually left the cottage at around two in the afternoon so he could take messages and make calls Sunday evening at his apartment. Like I said, he always liked to be prepared."

"Who would have been with him at the cottage?" I asked.

"That would have been a secret," she said. "He frequently took women friends there."

"You're going to have to straighten me out on my perception of Mr. Rudolph," Margo said. "Or maybe it's your perception. You say he wasn't the type to fool around, yet he took women to his cottage. Were they there alone?"

"Yes. I went with him a dozen times this year myself. He leaves the office at about one o'clock on Fridays—when possible—and a company driver runs him and a companion or two up to the cottage. All of his things are there. Leisure clothes, everything."

"What does he do for meals?"

"He cooks for himself, believe it or not."

Wally shook his head. "He could take an army of cooks up there."

"He could," Janell agreed, "but none who could cook like he could."

"But you're telling me that he was not romantically involved with any of these women?" Margo pressed.

"He wasn't with me, and he was very open. He would have told me who he was involved with, if he was. He never hid anything from me."

I knew what Margo was driving at. It just didn't compute. Either Janell was terribly naive, or Adrian Rudolph was a strange man. With a marriage on the rocks and many women at his beck and call, was it possible he was not involved with any? If he had been, we'd have had a headstart. Very often a mistress or an estranged wife is the best preliminary suspect.

"I hate to stay on this subject, Janell," Margo said, "but could you describe for me a typical weekend a woman might have with Mr. Rudolph?"

"Well, they were never typical, but he spent most of his time swimming and sunbathing and reading. When he was in the mood, we'd talk."

"That was it?"

"That was it. Some people resented that. They wanted to *do* something, anything. If he sensed that, they wouldn't be back."

"Did his wife ever go up there with him?"

"Only for big social events. We refer to it as a cottage, but you know it sleeps twelve."

"Would the chauffeur stay at the cottage?"

"Only at night. He was not to be there during the day unless Rudy told him in advance or called him from the little town."

"So Adrian Rudolph spent weekends with the women of his choice at a cottage in Wisconsin, yet he wasn't sleeping with them."

"Exactly," Janell said. "Their bedrooms would have been on opposite ends of the cottage."

"There were no staff people there at all?"

"Oh, yes. There are a couple of people who live there the year around, but when he was there on weekends, they were supposed to leave."

Wally had a puzzled expression. "This guy sounds weird—pardon the expression."

"It was just his way," Janell said. "I can't believe they bury him tomorrow. The funeral is at ten. Since I'm paying you to represent me, would it be all right if Philip escorted me?"

The three of us lurched as one. Margo was looking to me to decline, but Wally spoke before I could take a breath. "I'll escort you," he said. "Delighted. I'll use the funeral as a chance to get a bead on the various characters in this crazy play."

"We need to get one thing clear, Wally," I said. "Janell, are you saying that your boss was not electrocuted?"

"No, I'm sure he was. There seems little doubt of that. I'm just saying that it wasn't an accident. If there was faulty wiring in a cottage like that one, someone had to do it on purpose."

"And it had to be someone who knew the lay of the land and who also knew that Mr. Rudolph did his own lawn care."

"He didn't do his own lawn care. He just turned on the sprinkler system occasionally before leaving for Chicago. When his live-in people returned, they would shut it off."

"OK, let's get right down to it, Janell," Wally said, his mouth full. "You think his wife had reason to kill him?"

"I do. The marriage was bad, though they never separated."

"Except on weekends," Margo said.

Janell ignored her and continued. "Deirdre didn't much like his taking women up to the cottage on weekends and—as she put it—flaunting it. She clearly had designs on the company and pumped everyone but Rudy for information on what was going on. We learned to lie to her. She got her best information from Fred Towns, of course."

"Did Mr. Rudolph know of her relationship with Towns?"

"I told him more than once, but he pretended not to believe it or care one way or the other."

"Do you think he did care?"

"I don't know. I think it made him more eager to write her out of the will. But if it had been a real problem to him, he'd have fired Fred."

"And you think the timing of his death indicates that his wife had someone fix the wiring so it would kill him?"

"That's what I think."

"Why not this Manfred Towns? If he knew of the new will and the fact that his woman would take control of billions of dollars worth of assets, wouldn't he have a motive, too?"

"Yes, he sure would. Maybe they conspired to do it."

"Has Towns been to the cottage?"

"Oh, sure! Everybody in Rudy's orbit got up there once in a while. There were big parties occasionally, and if the cottage couldn't hold everyone, Rudy would spring for hotel rooms."

"Personal or business expense?"

"It's all the same. His expense account is bigger than your three salaries combined; I'd bet on that."

"What kind of money does a man like that make?" Wally said. "I ask that for more reasons than curiosity."

"I don't mind telling you. The amount makes for another motive for Deirdre, anyway. His salary was eight hundred and fifty thousand, but he also got a Mercedes and a chauffeur, health and life insurance, two residence allowances, and an unlimited expense account."

"By unlimited, you mean what?"

"For instance, he spent almost a hundred and fifty thousand last year from that account, no questions asked."

"What was your salary, if you don't mind my asking?" Wally said.

"I don't mind. Since three years ago, when he promoted me, he told me I would make five percent of his annual gross as long as I stayed with him. That's one of the nice things about my contract, too. It had a termination clause calling for a year's salary in a lump sum."

"His wife paid you a year's salary when she cut you loose?"

"That's right. But she overpaid me by about a thousand for some reason. Maybe Rudy was due for a small increase."

We all suppressed grins.

"More than forty thousand dollars a year for a secretary?" Wally said. "That boggles the—"

"I was *not* his secretary, Mr. Festschrift. I was his administrative aide, and there's a big difference."

"I'll bet there is," Wally said. "Probably around twenty-five big ones."

Margo glanced at her watch. "You'd better give us a quick education in mergers. Are these the types of things that the newspapers call 'hostile takeovers'?"

"Oh, I suppose. There's a lot of money involved, and once an offer has been made, there's little the target company can do about it. But it's all perfectly legal and aboveboard."

"How do the lawyers and banks get so much money out of it?"

"Well, they have the lion's share of work to do. It's all on paper. There's little negotiating, unless some other company tries to outbid you. Remember when DuPont took over Conoco a few years ago?"

"I guess I heard something about that."

"Mobil and Seagram's got into the act, and the bidding went sky high. DuPont finally won with an offer of seven and a half billion, and it cost them forty million in legal and bank fees alone."

We shook our heads.

"There are a lot of stories like that," she said. "Mobil and U.S. Steel bid against each other for Marathon Oil. U.S. Steel got it for six-point-two billion."

"Anytime there's that kind of money involved,

you've got trouble," Wally said. "But these hostile takeovers are fairly new, aren't they? I don't remember them from years ago."

"Oh, they used to carry more of a stigma than they do now. It's pretty much accepted anymore."

"By the buyer perhaps," Margo said. "But how does the seller feel with a gun to his head?"

Janell looked condescendingly at her and spoke slowly, as if explaining something to a child. "Not long after I got my M.B.A., Morgan Stanley and Company, a *very* reputable investment bank, represented International Nickel of Canada in a purchase of ESB, Inc. ESB was a battery manufacturer, headquartered in Pennsylvania. ESB fought it and said it was hostile and all that, and things got ugly, but with Morgan Stanley behind it, who could squawk? Everybody's been doing it ever since."

"Do you know exactly how it works and why?" Wally asked.

Janell laughed in his face. "Do I know? I majored in business and was administrative aide to one of the most powerful conglomeration CEOs in the country. The question is whether I could explain it so you could understand."

"Try me," Wally said.

Chapter Six

We returned to our offices, where Wally felt we'd be more comfortable and be able to take notes. "I'm gonna hafta put an eleven-thirty deadline on this," he said, looking at his watch. "I want my people home and in bed by midnight so they can be at it bright and early tomorrow. We've got two hours, a confident teacher, and three very bright pupils, Mrs. Barnard, so take us to school."

"Oh, where to begin?" Janell said, pacing before us like a prof as Wally reclined in a chair and Margo and I sat on desks, the three of us ready to write.

It was apparent that Janell's question was a rhetorical opening for her little lecture, but Margo has never been one for theatrics, and she had other reasons to have little patience with this performance. So, she answered her.

"Why not start with the reasons behind a hostile corporate attack on a smaller company?"

Janell stared at her, annoyed that she had been interrupted. "Oh, you *have* been studying this just a little, haven't you?" She began to say something else but stopped and turned to Wally. "You know, Mr. Festschrift, I really don't think this is a good idea. I'm convinced there is a lot I could teach you all about business and takeovers and everything, but I don't think we'll get any closer to the murderer of Mr. Rudolph."

Now it was clear Wally was upset. "I'll tell you what, dear," he said, "if you want to take us off the case, I'll hand you your check back and tell you it's been nice to meet you. It's not like we haven't got enough to do around here. But as long as we're representing you and you want us to move as quickly as possible on this case, you need to be available to give us whatever information we request. I told you that from the beginning. Your job is to tell us what we want to know, and our job is to decide which way to go with it. OK?"

She appeared properly rebuked. "OK," she said quickly. "The only person who would refer to a merger or a purchase or a buy out as a hostile attack would be the seller, in the event he's too shortsighted to see the value in selling."

"Now wait a minute," I said. "Isn't it true that an offer can be made to any public company at any time, whether it's up for sale or not?"

"Of course, and very often this takes the seller by surprise."

"You can't refer to an unwilling victim as the seller, can you?"

"Unwilling or not, if his shareholders agree to the sale, he's a seller, isn't he?"

"That certainly sounds hostile to me."

"It's American business. The free enterprise system. Welcome to the real world, Philip."

"So why does the big company or corporation or conglomeration want the little guy, anyway?" Margo asked.

"With high interest rates, it's cheaper for a corporation to buy a company that already has its manufacturing facilities, its research capabilities, and its resources in place than to start from scratch. The most expensive commodity in business used to be human resources, manpower, personnel, people. You know what it is now?"

"Money," Wally said.

"Money," Janell said.

Margo had a question. "What makes good smaller companies so lucrative? It seems if they were really good, they would be costly to a purchaser."

"That's a good question," Janell said, only slightly condescendingly. "During the past few years, investors have become wary of financing companies with vision and drive because those are the types of companies who take risks and try new things. I invest in companies like that, because I know the higher the risk the greater the reward. Everybody knows that, but few people are willing to take the risk.

"So, investors have been putting their money into more conservative, more popular, more interest-safe vehicles like money market funds. That means there's less money in the stock market as a whole, so prices start falling."

"So," Wally said, "the big guys, the ones who are cash rich, watch the markets carefully, and when a solid company sees a significant dip in its share value, they move in?"

"Right. Well, 'move in' might be a little strong, but admittedly, the prices are artificially low. Let's face it, the larger the gap between the price and the value, the more tempting the deal is for the shrewd buyer."

"In other words," Margo said, "kick them while they're down."

Janell smiled her knowing smile and said, "Well, perhaps bite them while they're down. The purchased company is usually the better for it. More capital is pumped in. New directions result."

"But if the company was doing well, why are new directions necessary, and where does the excess capital come from if it was spent purchasing the company?"

"If you're big enough to buy a multimillion dollar business, you're big enough to have something left over to invest in it."

"Is there any recourse to a victimized company?" I asked.

"Well, of course, I prefer not to refer to the seller as a victim, but no, there really isn't recourse. The more you fight, the noisier it becomes and the more bidders get into the picture. Then your advisers tell you to give it up, and your shareholders are interested in selling to the highest bidders. You see, many of the major shareholders bought in when the stock dropped, just hoping someone would offer them a better deal. They own low cost stock for a few months, then an angel comes in and makes them a cool profit."

"And you say the banks and lawyers do all right, too."

"Oh, sure. Even a failed bid, where the management of the seller matches the price or finds a friend to buy them out at a higher bid, nets the legal and financial community a quarter to a half million dollars in activity alone."

"You're kidding."

"You think that's good? That's a failure. In that DuPont takeover of Conoco, First Boston Corporation represented DuPont. Those few months worth of paperwork netted them fourteen million dollars."

"Bank and holding companies do as well as the purchaser then," I said, "for the amount of work involved."

"Even better, given the limited risk," Janell said.

I knew Margo was getting plenty to go on in her investigation at PlasTechs Limited, but I didn't know how all this business stuff would apply to my trip to Wisconsin. Yet Wally seemed intrigued. Up to a point.

About an hour later, he was yawning and suggesting that we probably had all we were going to get. While he was chatting with Janell, finding out where to pick her up for the funeral the next day, I moseyed up to Bonnie's desk and turned on the intercom.

When I returned, Margo was gathering up her things and Wally was heading for the door. "I'll see ya when you get back tomorrow, Philip," he said. "I'd like you to join Margo and me after lunch for a bull session and the other appointment."

"OK. Listen, Wally, do you mind if I use your office for a little while? I'd like to just reminisce with Janell for a few minutes."

"Sure. Just hit the lights and lock up when you leave."

Margo scowled at me, wondering what I was up to. "You don't mind, do you, dear?" I asked, overplaying it just a bit. "We won't be long."

She looked as if she wanted to say, "Yes, I *do* mind,

and what do you think you're trying to pull," but she simply sat down, as if willing to wait. Janell followed me into Wally's office, intrigued.

I shut the door and pointed to a chair. I sat in Wally's chair, and as I tidied up and moved a stack of files off to one side, I pressed his intercom button to the locked open position.

I could tell from the look on Janell's face that she thought our little private meeting was delicious. "I just thought we'd get reacquainted real quick," I suggested.

"That sounds lovely to me," she said.

"First, how long have you known I was in Chicago?" I asked.

"Since you first arrived, I guess. I was already working here when you came up from Atlanta on that murder case involving Margo's mother. I had sort of hoped you weren't romantically involved with Margo, but I was married at the time, anyway, so I decided not to look you up."

"That was wise."

"I'm not so sure. I lost you to her, didn't I?"

"I'm hers all right," I said. "But you lost me years ago."

"Perhaps, but I never gave up hope. Must I now?"

"Yes, you must. I couldn't be happier."

"Well, that's nice. My loss, but good for you."

"And did you come to EH because you knew we were a good agency who could help you out, or because I was here and you wanted to see if I was still available?"

"Uh, both. I admit it. Actually, they go hand in hand. I've read a lot about the agency and its reputation, and I hoped you were part of the reason it was so well known."

"I'm not. I started as a green trainee here under Earl Haymeyer, and he and Wally are the reasons this agency is what it is today."

"That's a nice, modest sentiment, but let me add that I knew the agency would be good and upright and straight with me, because you always were."

"I'm glad you think so. I always felt a bit of a scoundrel because of how we broke up."

"I think you handled it the only way you knew how. I was the scoundrel. I *am* the scoundrel."

"Why do you say that?"

"You don't think I am?"

"Ah, I don't think that's the first word I'd use in describing you."

"That was a nice political retreat. What *would* be the first word you would use to describe me?" She was smiling, figuring she had caught me and had forced me into a compliment I might not otherwise have proffered.

"Surprising," I said.

"Could have been worse. Why am I surprising?"

"You're not the same woman I knew in Columbus."

Her smile faded and she grew serious. "That's where you're wrong, Philip. And that's why I'm a scoundrel. The life I'm living now was the life I always dreamed of. I'm in business, at least I was. I will be again, and soon. I make a lot of money. I enjoy a lot of alimony from a man I never loved. I have everything I want."

"Everything?"

57

She paused and smiled. "Everything but you."

"You wouldn't want me, Janell. I don't fit that life-style in the least. Do you have any idea how little alimony you'd be getting from me if we'd been married and divorced?"

"That's not it, Philip," she said, fighting tears. "You were the only one who interrupted my ambition. I started at Ohio State with one goal in mind. Then I met you. You were different. You weren't rich. You weren't motivated by money. You cared about people and about God. All I could do was watch."

"But you were a Christian."

"I'd been taught that church was a good place for contacts, that's all. When you asked me if I had—what was it?—received Christ, I said yes because I didn't want you spending your whole college career trying to convert me. The truth was—and you probably knew it—that I could never get as excited about it as you and your friends were. I just couldn't. I still can't. And the worst part about it is that I know it's your faith that makes you attractive to me, that makes you different, that gives you that something I envy."

"You also know it's my faith that makes you off-limits to me."

"Oh, I know it, Philip. You don't have to remind me, and I won't embarrass you anymore."

"And you won't be cheeky to my wife?"

"No, I won't. She is truly lovely, you know."

"I noticed," I said.

And she smiled.

"Are you telling me that you never really gave up your career ambition?" I asked.

"I'm afraid not. I hid it well though, didn't I?"

"Yes. Especially after we broke up. I mean, I had noticed for a long time that you were not really into what I was into, but I never knew you were an out and out business tycoon type."

"You make that sound so terrible."

"Whatever makes your boat float. I guess it's as foreign to me as my life-style is to you."

"What did you think after we broke up?"

"I was sad," I said. "I missed you. Missed being with you, talking with you, being seen with you."

She brightened. "You did, huh?"

"Sure, I did. You knew that."

"I tried to be a good girl for you after that."

"But you were playacting."

"Yes, I was. And it was too late, wasn't it?"

I nodded. "It feels strange to know that you lived a lie for my sake."

"I was headed in the right direction, Philip."

"Yeah, I guess, but that makes me feel guilty, like I blew it and didn't see what was going on. I feel I've failed you somehow. Were you *ever* sincere? Like after we broke up?"

"No. I just wanted to do whatever was necessary to get you back. When that failed, I slipped very comfortably back into my real self."

"But what attracted you to me was not me!" I said. "It was God."

"Perhaps. But I had terrible plans, Philip. I wanted you, not your faith, not your church, not your lifestyle. If I could have had you, I was going to mold you into my type of person. And I would not have failed."

"The way I did, you mean?"

"If you want to put it that way."

"Why did I fail?" I asked.

"Because I was a lost cause from day one, that's why. I was determined not to be like you were. That's strange, isn't it? What you were attracted me to you, and you became a challenge. But I didn't want to be like you. I just wanted to own you, to make you mine, to change you."

"For the better?"

"For my sake, yes. Misery loves company. If you hadn't changed, I wouldn't have stayed with you any longer than I stayed with Bernard Barnard."

"What did you want from him?"

"A good marriage contract, and I got it."

"And you don't feel the least bit of remorse?"

She broke down and cried. "I feel worse about what I almost did to you," she said. "I would have turned you from something I wanted into something I could discard. It was a challenge."

"I was a challenge? That's all I was to you?"

She nodded miserably.

"And what would you have done with me if you had landed me this time around?"

"Probably the same, only with a different motive."

"What motive?"

"Revenge for dropping me."

"But you know why I did."

"Yes. But it still hurt."

"It hurt me too, Janell, and I want to apologize for any pain I caused you."

"I owe you a bigger apology than I can ever pay, Philip. I'm sorry, and I'm glad we were able to talk."

"One more question," I said. "What's your motive for finding the murderer of your boss?"

"The same."

"Revenge?"

"Revenge. Had I played my cards right, I might have gotten the company. Or the son. Same thing."

Chapter Seven

"You know," I said, rising, "that motive makes this investigation a little distasteful for all of us."

She shrugged and stayed seated. "You have a purer motive, I'm sure."

"If a murder was committed, regardless of the reason, we think the murderer should come to justice, yes."

"That's a purer motive all right," she said lightly, finally standing. "Use whichever motive you need, but solve it soon enough to stop the merger."

"None of us are that excited about the takeover, either, so that's an added incentive."

"Oh," she said, almost laughing. "Don't think I wouldn't pursue the same takeover if I ran the company, or influenced someone who did. It's a good move. Too good to let Deirdre get away with."

"Charming."

"Sorry to violate your principles, Philip."

"Are you sorry?"

"Nah. Had to say it though. I still try to maintain some dignity in conversation."

We moved toward the door. "Janell, if you ever get to the point where you listen to yourself, you might hear something you don't want to."

"One thing I know, Philip, is who I am and what I

am, and sometimes it hits me full force. But I'm basically comfortable with it."

"But occasionally it gets to you, doesn't it?"

"Like when?"

"Like when your boss dies, and you get fired, and everyone's sleeping with everyone else, and everybody's in the game for the money?"

"Maybe if I didn't have my own little challenge it would depress me. But investing in having your agency discover evidence that would put me back in the driver's seat—that I enjoy. It's difficult, and I need a few prescriptions, but I know I'm alive and that's what counts."

"You live for the battles?"

"Absolutely."

"And this is living?"

"It's all I know."

"No, it isn't. You know the alternative."

"Are you going to start in with your pitch, Reverend Spence?"

"C'mon, Janell. All I'm saying is that when your way leaves you bankrupt, you know where to turn."

She smiled a tolerant smile.

When we emerged from Wally's office, Janell said a quick good night to Margo to keep her from seeing that she had been crying. It was a good thing, because I could tell immediately that Margo had been crying too.

We turned out the lights and locked the door at 11:30 P.M. Margo was silent all the way to our apartment and even until we were almost ready to fall asleep. "Thank you, Philip," she said in the darkness. "I appreciated that very much."

"It was sad, though, wasn't it?"

"About the saddest thing I've heard since my mother died. But I'm glad you let me share it with you."

By nine the next morning I was cruising up Interstate 90 to Wisconsin's Lake Koshkonong with Wilbur "Stretch" Murphy in the shotgun seat, a heavy tool box on his lap.

"You can put it in the trunk, or even on the floor of the back seat," I had told him.

"Nope. This's fine."

He was fiftyish, long and knuckly, and his utility uniform was clean and pressed, as opposed to himself. A bit on the greasy side is the best way to say it. Fun to talk to, though.

He told me he worked for himself, used to employ three assistants, but never had enough patience with "a man who's slow or doesn't care about his work, and these three were both."

"You know Wally long?"

"Sarge? Yeah. Where you picked me up is right next door to where he used to live. His wife still lives there. His former wife, that is."

"I understand they may get back together."

"Yeah, that's what she's been tellin' my wife. That'd be good. They squabbled and everything, but they belong together. They couldn't raise them sons and get 'em outa there fast enough for my blood, though. Nobody, not even Sergeant F., deserves the grief those boys gave 'im. One of 'em's still behind bars. That's gotta embarrass an old cop, I 'magine."

"Wally says it's his fault, that he was never home long enough to be a good father or a husband."

Stretch swore. "Don't make no difference. Maybe he coulda been there more, but I don't buy this stuff says a no-good kid is his parents' fault. No sir, not even if Sarge says it."

When we got near the lake I located the nearest County Sheriff's Office and asked permission to visit the Rudolph residence. "No problem in the world with that," a deputy told me. "Place isn't off limits. I'd just go and knock on the door. There's a coupla servants in there'll probably let you in."

"The place isn't cordoned off for your evidence technicians?" I asked.

"We checked it out. No foul play."

"Did you take fingerprints?"

"When there's no foul play, pal, we don't care who's fingers' been where, know what I mean?"

I worried whether the help would let us in, since there'd been a murder and they were likely under orders from Mrs. Rudolph to keep people away. I called Janell. She told me I'd find a key near the birdhouse in the backyard, in case Ching wasn't in. We crept through the yard, and I unlocked the back door.

As we entered, a little Oriental man came running to the back staircase. I peeked back at Stretch, who was greatly enjoying the caper. "Electrician about your problem!" I hollered, and we trotted down the stairs. Ching said nothing, but I heard him hurrying across the floor and assumed he was going to the phone.

I pointed to where the outside water faucet led in

to the basement and told Stretch to get busy checking it out. It didn't look as if anyone had even been in the basement, but I knew they must have been in order to determine that Adrian Rudolph had been electrocuted.

I picked up the receiver of the extension phone and heard Ching asking for Mrs. Rudolph.

"She's not in right now, Ching," a woman's voice said. "What's the trouble?"

"Electrician here again," he said. "We no call electrician again."

"Maybe they're just checking to make sure everything's safe. So what?"

"They had key!"

"Then they must be from the power company. Don't worry about it, Ching! If they cause any trouble, call the cops."

I hung up when Ching did. He came carefully down the stairs and watched, so I started looking around and writing on a note pad. "Ah, Stretch," I said, "confidentiality is paramount here, pending repair to the vehicle."

Stretch slowly lowered his head from near a furnace duct and looked at me. "*What's* wrong with your car?" he asked.

I shook my head. "Delay your assessment until we've evacuated."

"I already paid my taxes," he said, incredulous. "What in the world are you yappin' about?"

Ching spoke up. "He try tell you don't say nothing till you outside."

We all laughed and Stretch continued poking around. After about twenty interminable minutes, with Ching still mutely staring from the landing, Stretch said, "Now all's I need is a piece of wire about this long." He held his hands a little less than a foot apart.

"You didn't bring any wire—?" I asked, but Ching skipped down the steps and past Stretch to a small wastebasket.

"Here one right here," he said. "Just found Sunday. Cleaning up before other electrician arrive."

"Thanks, buddy," Stretch said. "You got a cold glassa water?"

Ching headed for a utility sink and reached in a cabinet above his head.

"No, I mean with ice in it," Stretch said, puzzling me.

Ching ran upstairs. Stretch beckoned me with a gesture, then put his finger to his lips. He shined a flashlight up under a joist and motioned that I should hold the light. Then he wrapped the wire around the water line and showed how it perfectly reached the ground wire of the electrical system.

Ching was on his way down the stairs. I snapped off the light. Stretch thanked him for the water and asked where he had found the wire. Ching pointed near the sump pump, directly under where Stretch had shown me the hookup.

"Is that it for today, then, Stretch?" I asked.

"That's it."

"Thanks, Ching," we said in unison. He bowed. "You need this wire?" Stretch added.

Ching shook his head.

"Mind if I keep it?"

"No. You keep," Ching said, smiling.

Stretch nearly danced back to the car. He tossed his tool box in the back seat, jumped in front, and slammed the door, the wire clasped neatly in his left hand. "Hoo boy!" he said. "That was fun! I love detective work, an' I'm good at it, ain't I?"

"I guess, except for not understanding me when I was trying to talk over Ching's head."

"I understood you perfectly, son. I just could tell that ol' Ching did too, so I wanted to play dumb so's he'd prove it to you and you wouldn't tell him nothin' he wasn't s'posed to know. Know what I mean?"

"Are you serious?"

"'Course I'm serious; what'dya think—I can't understand high falutin' English?"

I didn't know what to think. "So what do you make of the wire?"

"How'd you like the way I got ol' Ching outa there for a minute? Pretty slick, huh? You ever pull somethin' like that? 'Course you have. You was pretty slick there yerself, gettin' in with that key and that line of yours. I noticed you didn't lie."

"You did, huh? I never do, and that makes my job pretty difficult sometimes. Now, what'd you find, Stretch?"

"Well, the only new wirin' done in that basement lately is a new connector and cap where the ground wire runs into the box. Everything else is as usual. So I figure, knowin' what you're lookin' for, that someone who knew what they was doin' disconnected that ground wire and put in a temporary short-cut. They grounded the power to the water line that leads outside. First guy touches that faucet head is a dead man, which is, I know, what happened.

"Now, unless Ching done it hisself, which I don't think so 'cause he coulda got rid o' the wire, whoever done it got down in there and yanked that wire off there again. Now I'm just guessin' after this, but I'm bettin' whoever it was heard people comin' and they just dropped that wire and didn't have time to hook the ground wire up proper again."

"Why do you say that?"

"Well, it was just a long shot that that wire would still be around there somewhere. I couldn't believe my eyes when ol' Ching come hoppin' through there and give it to me. But here's the thing: If the person who done it was gonna cover his tracks, he woulda got that wire down offa there and hooked the ground wire up proper again, only he didn't. So when the cops come lookin', all they see is the ground wire still unattached, figure it's come loose from vibrations or somethin'—which happens now and again—and they have somebody come in and replace the end of the wire and the cap."

"I'm amazed," I said.

"I like this kinda work," he repeated.

"You ought to. You're good at it. Guess that's why Wally recommended you."

"Oh, he'll be prouda me, won't he?" Stretch said, cackling. "Hoo, that was fun! But don't kid yerself. Ol' Sarge recommended me cause he knew there wasn't another spark man would do it for five hunnert bucks."

"Four hundred," I said.

He flashed a toothy grin. "Can't blame me fer tryin'."

And I decided to see if I couldn't talk Wally into an

extra C-note for Stretch, especially if we could use the evidence. I wished I'd stayed and shot a few pictures and learned the layout of the house, but I figured maybe Janell would know the floor plan well enough to tell where someone would escape from the basement to elude anyone coming through the back.

"Anything else I should know about that wire? I don't suppose there's a chance of getting any fingerprints from it now, after you and Ching have handled it."

"Nope, but you wouldn't have, anyway."

"Why not?"

"If the guy had touched it with a bare hand, he'd be dead too. See here? This is bare wire. Had to be wearin' gloves when the juice was on. Way I figure it, the juice was always on or it would have tipped off everybody in the house, 'cause all the lights and appliances go off."

"I can't believe what you can tell from one little piece of copper wire, Stretch," I said, making him beam.

"There's more," he said. "But I don't know if it's important or not."

"Let me hear it. You're on a roll."

"See the ends of this wire?" He held it up to my face. I tucked my chin to my chest to get a look at them.

"Yeah, but I'm not an electrician."

"Neither was the person who cut this wire, I'm guessin'. Either that or they don't know how to use cutters. This piece of wire was not cut the way you do it—one clean snip—if you know what you're doin'. It was cut with a tool, all right, and likely wire cutters,

70

but you can tell from the ends that it was done by just holdin' the wire in the teeth of the cutters and bendin' it back and forth till it busted. See what I mean?"

I saw. But I didn't know what it meant.

Chapter Eight

After lunch, when I dropped Stretch off at his home, I told him he'd be getting a check within a few days.

"That means I'll have to report it," he said.

"Report it?"

"On my IRS."

Back at the office, Wally and Margo and Janell were finishing a fast food lunch, being careful not to spill on their finery. Janell had been crying.

I told them about the laxity of the sheriff's office in securing the crime scene.

"First of all," Wally said, "they apparently didn't view it as a crime, just an accident."

"But still," I said, "they might have—"

Janell was shaking her head and holding up an index finger, waiting to speak until she had swallowed. "That's not it at all," she said. "Mid-America owns that sheriff. Fifteen thousand to his campaign fund four years ago and the same early this year. If anyone on the lake calls in a complaint about the cottage, the deputies come out and give the *complainant* a hard time. Those deputies found what they wanted to find in that basement."

"Who found the body?" I asked.

"The chauffeur. He showed up with Ching to take Rudy back, but they couldn't find him in the house. His bag was packed, and that morning's *Tribune* was blowing around in the backyard, so he apparently was ready to go. He probably left the paper on the deck and went to turn the sprinkler on."

Wally was scribbling notes again. "He have a car up there?"

"No."

Wally stood and moved toward his office, motioning me to follow. "Get on the horn," he said, "and find out from the county coroner up there how long Rudolph was dead by the time they found him. Also, find out who delivers a morning paper to those cottages. But hurry. We've got a two o'clock appointment at PlasTechs."

"It was murder, Wally," I said. "I didn't figure you wanted me to say anything in front of Janell." I told him what Stretch had discovered and pulled the wire from my pocket. Wally nodded slowly and left me to my phone call.

By the time I got out of Wally's office, Janell had left and Margo and Wally were ready to get in the car. "Tell me about the funeral," I said as we rode to the west side of Chicago.

"You first," Wally said. "What'd you learn?"

"Coroner says he was called by the sheriff at one-thirty and arrived about twenty minutes later. The body was still warm, and other indications led him to believe that death had occurred within the hour. The deputies had first assumed it was a heart attack, but the coroner noticed that the fingers were still wrapped around the faucet head. He sent the cops downstairs

73

to look around, and one of them noticed the ground wire was unattached. The three of them, the two deputies and the coroner, deduced that the connector had worked loose because of vibrations over the years, and the sheriff sent out an electrician immediately. Of course, we happen to know that by then, the housekeeper, a man named Ching, had tidied up in the basement to the point where all the evidence was ruined."

"Not all," Wally said. "I told Margo about the wire. Something else is sticking in my craw. Unless whoever did this was very careful and *wanted* it to appear that the ground wire had merely shaken loose, it seems there would be some damage to the ground wire or the connector or the box. Was there?"

"Well, the connector was new, and the cap was new."

"Then maybe that cord was yanked rather than just carefully loosened. If you wanted to make it look like an accident, wouldn't you unscrew the cap just enough to free the wire, then tighten the cap a little again?"

"I guess."

"Then all a person would have to do to repair it is to slip the wire back in and tighten it down real good."

"Maybe the electrician figured a new connector and cap would ensure its not shaking loose again."

"I'm sure, Philip, but if you can get to that electrician and find out if there was damage to that ground wire, we've got even more to go on."

"I may have to go up there again?"

"You may."

74

"How much knowledge of electrical things would a person have to have to pull off something like that?" Margo asked. "I consider myself reasonably intelligent, and I can fix things around the house, but I wouldn't know the first thing about ground wires and all that."

"Then you're not a suspect," Wally said.

"I'm serious," she said. "Are we looking for someone who knows a lot about electricity?"

"I don't know," I said. "I guess they'd have to have some rudimentary knowledge to keep from killing themselves in the process. I don't think I could have figured out that whole thing and made it work."

"Me either," Wally said. "So, once again Mrs. Sherlock Holmes helps us arrive at one of the first characteristics of the murderer. Someone who has at least a rudimentary knowledge of electricity and wiring."

"Don't call me Mrs. Sherlock Holmes," Margo said. "You know what that makes Philip."

"Cute," I said.

"Let's try to recreate the scene," Wally said. "If we can picture the sequence in our minds, it'll help us when we interview at PlasTechs. Janell says it's a secret who Rudolph went to the cottage with, but we've got to find out from the driver, because it's unlikely anyone else knows. I'll try to handle that. Now, we assume Rudolph was up there with someone. The servants were gone, as was the custom unless there was a big party. The weekend is over, the chauffeur is on his way back, and he brings Ching with him. Whoever is with Rudolph has to find some reason to be in the house when Rudolph is outside, ready

75

for his paper and to watch the sprinklers from the deck. Where'd he get that paper, Philip?"

"According to the coroner, who admitted that newspaper buying is a bit far afield from his area of expertise, the local rag is delivered, but not the *Tribune*. He said it would not have been delivered unless Rudolph arranged it with someone. The closest place to get a Chicago paper is at a little store at the end of the drive that goes around the lake."

"He could have gotten the Sunday *Tribune* the night before, couldn't he?" Margo asked.

I nodded, but Wally said no. "Around here you could have, but one of the reasons they produce them so early is so they'll have time to get them up to little outposts like that. I'm guessing that paper was bought that morning, and since Rudolph had no wheels, someone brought it to him. We need to know who. Philip, you've got a list for your next trip up there, don't you?"

"Yeah, and I s'pose I should go again late this afternoon."

"You got it, Sherlock."

"Can I go too?" Margo asked.

"Let's see how things go here. Maybe you can."

"Are you gonna tell us about the funeral, Wally?"

"Oh, yeah, it was somethin' else. Like a who's who. Lots of important people. Lots of dignitaries I recognized. City officials, people like that. I was glad I had Janell with me, 'cause she was able to tell me who all the people were from the Mid-America headquarters. We drew a lot of stares though, 'cause she kept wantin' to hang onto my arm. People kept greeting her and asking her if I was her dad."

"What does Mrs. Rudolph look like?"

"A little different than what I imagined. She dresses well, of course, and Janell was right about the black veil and all. She played it up like she was the first lady of the US or somethin' and we'd just lost the president. She's a tall gal, and kinda hefty, but she has that same aura of power that Adrian Rudolph must have had."

"Was she escorted by the lawyer?"

"Towns? No. She was with her son and two daughters and their husbands."

"Was she sad?"

"Hard to tell. She looked stunned, that's all, but that could have been put on if we can believe Janell."

"I'm sure she *was* stunned," Margo said. "Even if she hated the man and was out to take his money and his company, the truth of his death had to hit her hard, if not Monday or Tuesday, surely today at his funeral."

"You're forgetting one thing," Wally said. "She may have murdered him."

Margo thought for a moment. "That may be," she said. "But I'll bet there would still be the shock of reality when she's sitting there staring at his body in the casket."

"Who was Towns with?" I asked.

"He had a woman on his arm who looked quite a bit younger than he was, but not to the point of scandal. She could have passed for a wife of ten years younger, but Janell said it was a woman from the office. All for show, Janell said."

"What's he look like?"

"Like a lawyer."

We laughed.

"Well, you know what I mean," Wally said. "Sharp dresser, conservative, kinda stiff and outa shape. Must be fifty at least."

"He kept his distance from Deirdre and the family?"

"Totally."

"Interesting."

"Sure was."

"Anybody else there we should know about?"

"Let's see. Most of the others were just people from the office, all playing up to the new boss. Oh, the other lawyer, ah, Rudolph's personal lawyer, and his wife were there."

"Zack something?"

"Yeah, Zachary Hayes and, um, Theresa or Terri or something like that."

"I wonder how he feels," Margo said, "after being cut out of the merger and now cut out of all future stuff because of the death of his client."

"Would you believe it?" Wally said. "I swear if I didn't know better, the man gave his business card to the widow, just like an ambulance chaser."

"Surely not," Margo said. "Right in front of everyone?"

"Yes!"

"Maybe it was a message or a sympathy card or something."

"I'm tellin' ya, it looked like a business card. Janell even remarked about it."

"Hard to believe."

"Yeah, maybe, but I think his wife put him up to it. She just had that look about her. They're young, ya know, you kids' age. Maybe thirty, but not much more."

"And his wife seemed strange to you?"

"Sniveling, you know? Kind of a scrunched up, pointy face in a cutesy sort of way, except she looks like the cynical type. I gotta think she pushes this kid, Zack, unmercifully. Here's a guy who advised his client on cutting his wife out of his will, and now he's givin' the widowed wife his business card? I mean, come *on!*"

"You think his wife knows about the new will?"

"Oh, yeah! If Janell has a copy, there's got to be something on it in Rudolph's papers, and you know this Deirdre and Manfred Towns have been through everything already to make sure she's gonna get everything she's got coming to her."

"If she's guilty," Margo said, "I hope we're committed to the same."

"Yeah," Wally said. "That's good! I like that! Hey, I just remembered who else was there. How could I forget? What's his name, Janell's husband!"

"Bernard Barnard?" I said.

"Ol' Beebee himself. What a loser! Guess who he was there with? His mother! What a pair! He's a real wimp."

"Wally!" Margo scolded. "How do you know that?"

"Because he greeted Janell, looked me up and down, and then shook my hand when Janell introduced us. It was like shakin' hands with a bowl of Jello. Ooh, a wimp!"

"That doesn't make him a wimp, Wally."

"Call it what you want. I'd rather shake hands with

an old lady. He was prissy and fussy. And rich? I was low man on the shekels totem pole at that gatherin', I'll tell you that."

We fell silent as Wally pulled into the parking lot of PlasTechs Limited on the West Side. It was hard to believe this factory and office complex was located within the city limits of Chicago. It was gorgeous.

The road leading to the reception center was immaculate. The grounds were pin neat, freshly mowed, artistically landscaped. The buildings were attractive.

When we entered the lobby we read a moveable-type sign: Welcome Today to Mr. Festschrift and Mrs. and Mrs. Spence, the EH Co. We were greeted by the receptionist who took us to a conference room where we were to wait for someone to come and escort us to the president's office.

"You're in luck today," she said. "His wife is in helping with a project."

"And her name?" Wally asked.

"Jeane. You'll like her."

"Thank you. I'm sure we will," he said.

The employees we noticed in the hallways were dressed up. Shirts and ties on the men and dresses or skirts and blouses on the women. "Reminds me of IBM," I said.

"If this guy runs his business the way he cares for his buildings and grounds," Margo said, "I can see why someone would want to buy it."

"Sets high standards," I said. "Did you see those performance plaques for employees all over the walls? Seems to care about morale."

"Cares about business and the bottom line," Wally said, expressionless. "And he could be a murderer."

Chapter Nine

"Forgive the delay," Vincent Moorehouse said, rising as we entered his office. "I had to roll the sleeves back down, tighten the tie, and put the coat back on. This is my wife, Jeane, and she's been helping me pack."

We all shook hands with Jeane and couldn't help but notice the quiet confidence of the company president and his wife. He was on the young side of forty, trim and in terrific shape with good color and a firm grip. He wore lightweight grey slacks, a fabric belt, light blue Ivy League button-down shirt, navy club tie with gold stripes, and navy blazer. She was only slightly lesser dressed, more for packing than receiving guests.

"I think I'll excuse myself now," she said, but her husband interrupted.

"Oh, please stay," he said. "I think it will be all right with Mr. Festschrift and his people."

"Of course," Wally said. He loved a challenge.

"I'm at your disposal for up to forty minutes," Moorehouse said. "Please feel free to refer to us by our first names, and ask whatever you would like."

"Thank you. OK, Jeane, just to fill you in, we're investigating the death of Adrian Rudolph, president of—"

"I know perfectly well who he is," she said with a sweet smile. "And you assume because our company has been victimized by his that my husband may have had something to do with his death."

"Oh, my, no," Wally said. "We haven't come to that conclusion at all. Your husband is naturally someone we were very eager to interview, and you too, ma'am, but we have not begun to suspect anyone yet."

"Then why are your here and what do you want?" She was still smiling.

"Do I have the freedom too to ask you whatever I want, as your husband said?"

"Certainly."

"Then my question is yours."

"I'm sorry?"

"Why are you here and what are you doing?"

"I don't see how that pertains—"

"Well, of course it pertains, Mrs. Moorehouse—Jeane. You immediately went on the defensive when you learned we were investigating the suspicious death of a man you undoubtedly do not care for, so let me ask you what are you packing and where are you going?"

"Vincent has lost his job as of Friday, and we are simply cleaning out his office."

"I see. Is this common in such a purchase—to fire the president of the selling company?"

"Let me make one thing very clear," Vincent said, "this company was not bought; it was stolen. You can see for yourself, and I'll be happy to give you a tour of the facilities, that we have something here to be proud of. We, the team, the employees, have built this place from a small manufacturer of plastic toy parts to a multimillion dollar corporation, a leader in the plastics industry. We lost an account with one of the major toy manufacturers—and please ask me why—and suddenly our stock took a temporary tumble. Within days I was informed of the tender by Mid-America. I was sick. I'm still sick."

"OK, Vincent," Wally said, "I'm asking why you lost the account with the big toy manufacturer."

"Because we insisted on higher standards for his product than he did. He asked for a better price, so we showed him where all the costs were incurred and asked him if he thought our profit expectation was unreasonable. He agreed quickly that it was not and suggested we sharpen our pencil, not in the area of our margin, but in hard costs."

"In other words, cut the quality."

"Precisely."

"And you refused."

"Of course."

"So who lost whom?"

"Excellent question, Mr. Festschrift. My sentiments exactly."

"If I can return to my original question, Vince," Wally said, drawing a grimace from Mrs. Moorehouse, who apparently had not heard her husband referred to as Vince for at least a decade, "Is it common in a deal like this—a theft if you prefer—to fire the president of the victimized company?"

"Not always," Moorehouse said. "In fact, in a case such as this one, where the seller is quite healthy, it's more common to leave the management structure in place, while adding a key member from the new parent corporation to the board of directors."

"So what happened here?"

"Mrs. Rudolph happened here," Jeane said.

Vincent Moorehouse was visibly upset with his wife now. "I wonder, dear, if you wouldn't mind waiting outside for me. And please ask Ethel to have Hayes step in."

She turned red and appeared on the verge of tears. She left without a word.

"You don't mind if I have counsel here, do you?" Moorehouse asked. And then he laughed. "I really don't care whether you mind because I want to have counsel when we get into the specific questions about our relationship with Mid-America."

"In that case," Wally said, also smiling, "I don't mind. Can you tell me what you feel is wrong with a big corporation taking over a smaller one? Not necessarily how you feel in this personal situation, but in general?"

"Sure. I agree with most economists who believe that management freedom, the kind that results in innovation and creativity, is lost when the big boys take over. Even if I were to stay here, I would have to pass every major decision through the hierarchy of Mid-America, and anything that didn't fit in with their overall, conservative game plan, related to their worldwide holdings, would be scuttled. I'd go crazy."

"But you would have stayed."

"For a time. I'm a reasonable man. I'm an entrepreneur, but I am very analytical. I would have given the thing a chance. Perhaps Mid-America would have proved me happily wrong. They were going to pay me handsomely to stay and find out."

"They were?"

"I was offered a forty percent increase in salary to stay on for a year, to be renegotiated annually."

"And?"

"I took it."

"But now you're leaving."

"The original offer came from the dead man himself, Adrian Rudolph."

"Your wife said something about Mrs. Rudolph."

"Correct, and now I prefer to wait until my counsel arrives—oh, here he is now. Come in, Zack. Zachary Hayes, these people are investigating Mr. Rudolph's death."

I was glad I wasn't in mid-conversation when he walked in. I wouldn't have been able to continue. Wally handled it famously, though I could tell he was just as shocked.

"Very nice to meet you," Hayes said. "May I ask who you are representing?"

"I am not at liberty to tell you that, Mr. Hayes, but as my associate Mrs. Spence here told Mr. Moorehouse's people on the phone yesterday, we do not represent Mid-America or anyone employed by them. Is that sufficient?"

"Yes, please proceed."

"And how is Terri?" Wally pressed.

"Excuse me, sir?"

"Your wife, Theresa. How is she?"

"She's fine, thank you," he said evenly. "Do you know her?"

"Not really, no. I'm just aware of her, shall we say?"

"From where?"

"A recent social gathering."

"I see."

And Zachary Hayes was silent. Wally asked anything and everything he wanted, and when it appeared that Zachary was about to protest and advise Moorehouse not to answer, Wally just stared him down, as if daring him.

"If I may continue," Wally said, "is it not true that more capital can be pumped into a company like yours if a large conglomerate takes it over?"

"That's a myth too," Moorehouse said, warming to the subject. "The fees that Mid-America had to pay to lawyers and banks had to bite into their budgeted amounts of spending money for the new company, and that has to reduce the earnings and the monies available for new investment. Our cash reserves have been depleted by trying to defend ourselves in this, which merely made our value go down more. That's why I was counseled not to fight it."

"By whom?"

"By my advisers."

Wally turned to Zachary Hayes. "Boy, with all that money going to lawyers, Mr. Hayes, I'll bet you wish you'd been on the other side of this one, getting a piece of that action, huh?"

Hayes squirmed. "Well, heh, heh," he said, "you know, ha, under the circumstances . . ."

"Yeah, I know," Wally said. "Lovely service today, wasn't it?"

87

"Yes, yes it was. My wife and I represented Plas-Techs, you know. Did I see you there?"

"I don't think so," Wally said. "I was there, but I don't think you saw me. How long have you been with PlasTechs now, Mr. Hayes?"

"Just a few days," Moorehouse broke in. "And we've really appreciated his counsel."

"I want to get back to what happened to your deal with Mid-America, Vince, and then I'll ask you more about how Mr. Hayes has helped you."

Hayes squinted at Moorehouse, but Wally stared him down.

"Well, it was quite simple," Vincent said. "As I told you, the original offer came from Mr. Rudolph himself, and I don't mind telling you, as bitter as I have been about this merger, I was impressed. I mean, Adrian Rudolph calling me? There was no protocol demanding that. My wife and I were tempted to call *him* at times, and my guess is they would have patched us through, but I was flattered that he himself would make contact. All the rest of the communications had been through intermediaries and seconds."

"And he made what you felt was a generous offer."

"Yes, and frankly, I felt it was a wise move. He was very direct with me, very open. He said he knew I had to be hurting and that I was probably thinking about trying to find a white knight, and so he—"

"Excuse me?" Wally said. "A white knight?"

"Right. It's a rescuer, a friendly company who can afford to outbid the kidnapper, the corporation who made the first offer. They really have no reason to buy, weren't in the market, but are sympathetic and will do it as an act of protest against the Goliath. Of course, I would submit to a shotgun marriage like that in a minute. Shoot, I'd sooner merge with a garbage company than a hostile conglomeration. See what I mean?"

Wally nodded.

"In fact," Moorehouse added, looking to Hayes who sat up straight in his chair, "that is one of the areas that Zack here has tried so diligently to pursue."

"Merging you with a garbage collector?" Wally said, laughing.

Moorehouse cackled too. "No, finding us a white knight."

"You accepted Rudolph's offer, yet you were still looking for a rescuer?"

"I'm sorry, I'm getting ahead of myself. We've been looking for a rescuer only since Monday when the call came from Mrs. Rudolph."

"OK, good, now we're back to her."

"Well, not exactly, and that was my point in emphasizing that I heard directly from *Mr.* Rudolph at the time of the original offer. I heard from him. I never heard from her. I heard from her lawyer, ah, Mr., ah—"

"Towns," Zachary Hayes said, "Manfred Towns."

"Right. You see, to finish my story about Mr. Rudolph, he was pretty sensitive. He guessed exactly where my head was. He said he knew I would be afraid of what might happen to my company and my own career, though he was kind enough to say that he was sure I would land on my feet somewhere. But he wanted me to know that his hope was that I would

continue as president of PlasTechs and that his desire
was that he himself be the major contact person. That
was all I needed to hear, and I was feeling better
about the deal already, though I wasn't sure how
much I could trust Rudolph. Then he offered to
sweeten the pot, salarywise, and I told him that
wasn't necessary."

"You did?"

"I was serious. I didn't want to feel that I was
being bought off. My people had heard rumors of a
takeover, and they kept demanding to know if I was
going to let it happen. Well, I didn't have any
recourse, but I certainly didn't want to get rich in
the process. So I was toying with the idea of staying
on and either declining or at least deferring the salary increase. Then I made my major mistake. I told
the employees that the takeover was imminent and
that I wanted them to do me a favor and get used to
it and welcome it. I told them it wasn't necessarily
the first choice of anyone at PlasTechs, but that we
were all going to make the best of it. I told them I
thought Adrian Rudolph was an honorable man and
that he wanted me to stay, and that I would on one
condition: that they promise me they would continue to perform at their highest level and settle for
nothing but the best."

Recounting the experience had nearly left Moorehouse in tears.

"How did they respond?" Wally asked softly.

Moorehouse's lip quivered, and he clenched his
teeth to keep from crying.

"Standing ovation," Zachary broke in.

Wally looked with disdain on the lawyer, who

immediately looked away. "So, Vince, when Mrs. Rudolph's attorney called . . ."

"He told me I would be given six month's severance pay and that I was to be out of the office by the time of the official takeover—that would be the day after tomorrow. I was speechless. I asked if he was aware of the arrangement I had with Mr. Rudolph, and he asked me if I had it in writing. I said no, and he informed me that Mr. Rudolph had passed away and that he was speaking on behalf of the new president of the company, Mrs. Rudolph."

"Which is illegal," Zack Hayes said, "because the stipulations of the will would not go into effect that quickly anyway."

"Which is irrelevant," Vincent said, without apologizing to Hayes. "She's going to inherit the job, and if she doesn't want me, she doesn't want me. So, I'm clearing out. Oh, yes, I did tell Towns what he could do with the severance pay."

"You did, huh?" Wally said with a guffaw.

"I shouldn't have. It was beneath me, but I didn't want it."

"They will send it anyway," Hayes said.

"And I will divide it up between the people who have made this place what it is."

Suddenly Wally stood. "I'm going to do something I don't normally do, Mr. Moorehouse. I'm going to ask my people something in front of you. I've been guilty of some theatrics in the past, they can attest, but I've never pulled this. I'm going to ask them individually, and I want them to answer without hesitation, because they have formed certain opinions in listening here. Philip, I want to know if you believe this man and everything he has said here today?"

"Well, uh, yeah," I said. "Yes, I do."

"And you, Margo?"

Chapter Ten

"Absolutely," she said, the look on her face making it clear she was worried where Wally was headed.

"Thank you," Wally said. "I may be making a huge error here, but I must tell you, Mr. Moorehouse, I agree with my people."

"Well, thanks for not calling me a liar, I guess," Vincent said.

"That's not my point," Wally said, still standing. "I'm impressed with you and your abilities. I like your style. I like what you've done with this company. I like the way you treat your employees, and I think you're a loyal, ethical man."

"Thank you."

"Don't thank me. I'm not finished. I do, however, feel you have made a serious error. In your pain, and for the sake of you and your wife and your family and your people, you have made an error in judgment that I would like to save you from. I probably wouldn't do it if I didn't believe you, and let me say, you're almost a little too good to be true. If I didn't have a couple of super straight shooters on my own staff, I wouldn't think people like you really existed. So let me tell you that your lawyer here, Mr. Hayes, is not worthy of you. You should have known better, Mr. Moorehouse, than to listen to the first rescuing lawyer to hit your doorstep after a buy-out offer has been made."

"But company mergers and rescuing the victims are his area of expertise!"

"Wrong. Opportunism is his area of expertise. He's a highly paid ambulance chaser. You were hurt and he was there. You chose him, Mr. Moorehouse, and you can choose to dump him."

"You happen to be on dangerous ground related to slander, Mr. Wally or whatever your name is!" Hayes shouted.

"Just calm down, Zack," Moorehouse said. "No one is going to put you down in my presence without all the facts. Now what's your point, Mr. Festschrift?"

"I think Mr. Hayes should tell you who his most recent personal client was."

"I have many," Hayes said, "and they are confidential. None of your business."

"But one of them, recently deceased, *is* Mr. Moorehouse's business, is he not?"

"I am not limited to the number of clients I can represent, sir. Mr. Moorehouse is fully aware that I represent many people from many walks of life."

"But you *are* limited as to how many sides of the same case you may represent, are you not?"

Hayes glared at him.

"What is he saying, Zack?" Moorehouse asked. "I want to hear it from you."

"He doesn't know what he's talking about, Vince. I'm not representing two sides of any issue, I swear."

"No, you're not now," Wally said. "Because your other client died Sunday."

"Zack!" Moorehouse said. "Tell me you weren't Adrian Rudolph's lawyer!"

Hayes just continued staring at Wally, silent. Moorehouse held his head in his hands and said, "That explains a few things, doesn't it, Zack?"

Hayes didn't respond.

"That explains why you didn't want me to go to Rudolph's party on Friday, the thirteenth. You said it was bad luck, not a good idea, and all the rest. You said it wouldn't look right. But you knew better, didn't you? *You* wanted to go. *You* were there. And if I went, you couldn't go. And if I happened to drop your name, everything would have come crashing down around you, wouldn't it?"

Hayes stomped to the door. "Let me just say this," he said, his voice quavering, "I wasn't representing Mid-America in the takeover! I represented Rudolph, yes, but only on personal matters. I didn't approach you until I was told clearly that I would not be involved in the takeover litigation."

"Oh, that makes it all better," Moorehouse said. "That's just wonderful, Zack, my friend, my rescuer. You couldn't get in on the big pot of gold so you thought you'd come my way for a little silver. I've got news for you. You try to collect a penny for the services you've rendered here and I'll have you up before the bar so fast your head will swim."

Wally sat again when Hayes was gone and just looked at the ashen Moorehouse.

"Whew!" Moorehouse said. "Here I thought you were going to tell me I was a murder suspect, and I was going to tell you that if the dead person was Mrs. Rudolph you may have come to the right place. I can't figure any of this anymore. You think Zack was a spy?"

"Oh, no, no," Wally said. "He's as much on the outs over there as he is here. He was representing Adrian Rudolph in action against his wife. He wanted a piece of the merger action and Rudolph told him maybe next time. You assessed it right. He came to get what he could get."

"Well, thank you. That's all I can say."

In the parking lot back at our office, Wally made the assignments for the evening. "You're both still up to this, right? I mean, I know it's askin' a lot."

We agreed we were still excited about the case. "You've already got your double fee in the bag, don't you, Wally?" Margo asked. "Certainly you have enough by now to stop the merger."

"Probably, but I'm less inclined to look for the murderer on the victimized company side of the street now. It looks like an inside job, doesn't it?"

We nodded.

"OK, you'd better get up to that lake with the crazy name as soon as you can. Luckily, we've got plenty of daylight remaining. I don't care which of you handles what, but I need everything you can get from the electrician who made the minor repairs in that basement, from anyone at that little store who remembers who bought a Sunday *Tribune* that morning, from neighbors who saw who was there, whatever. I'm guessing now that the murder took place just moments before the chauffeur and Ching returned to the cottage that afternoon, maybe as they were arriving."

"Why?"

"Because of what Stretch said about dropping the wire and not reattaching the ground connection. It makes sense, doesn't it? Whoever did this heard the front door opening and Ching and the chauffeur walking through the house, and knew he had to get out. I'll be asking Janell where someone would go to escape in a situation like that."

"Could Ching and the chauffeur have done it?"

"It's possible, except they probably would have been more careful about covering their trail. They wouldn't have just dropped the wire and not reattached the other one. And surely Ching would not have been so helpful with Philip and Stretch. Of course, we're not aware of any motive for either of them, either, but we don't know."

"What will you be doing, Wally?"

"I'm going to visit the chauffeur, and to get Janell to give me the floor plan and possible way of escape, as well as the complete list of who was at the Friday night party the week before. I'll spend the rest of the day today and all day tomorrow getting background information on every person at that party. Something tells me our murderer had to have been there."

"That'll keep you busy."

"Yeah, probably till late tonight. I'll see you guys here at eight in the morning."

While Margo was quizzing the clerk at the small store at the end of the road that went around the lake, I used the pay phone to call a couple of local electricians. I located the one who admitted having done the work at the Rudolph place, and he agreed to see me.

"Bizarre," Margo said in the car.

"What? What?"

"The kid who clerks here says the only person outside of the locals he remembers selling a *Tribune* to last weekend was Adrian Rudolph's son, Keith."

"His *son?*"

"Yeah, but don't make too much of it yet. It was *Saturday* evening, and he sold him the last Saturday paper he had in the store. I asked him if he remembered anything unusual about the man. He said no, just that he seemed awfully tired, as usual, and—also as usual—he was driving a beautiful black sports sedan. The kid doesn't remember the make or model, but he always admires it. Thinks it's European."

"That's it?"

"That's it."

"We don't know if the son was on his way here or on his way home."

"Oh, the kid definitely said he was heading away from here when he stopped for the paper, but who knows what that means?"

"We'd better call the office and put the message on the answering machine, because Wally should know that the son was up here, at least on Saturday."

"Right, and that he drove himself."

After the call, I dropped Margo off in the neighborhood of the Rudolph cottage to go door to door and see what she could learn. She loves that kind of thing. I do it, but I hate it. I sort of hoped she would be finished by the time I returned, but it was unlikely.

I found the Wayne Reber home about a mile up the road from Rudolph's, just as he said I would. Reber was a retired handyman, "only listed in the book as an electrician because that's the only thing people want a handyman to do anymore."

"Who called you to handle this job?" I asked.

"Sheriff."

"When was this?"

"Sunday afternoon last. They were afraid the electricity might jump again from the ground wire to the pipes. Wasn't going to happen, though. That was kind of a freak thing in my book. Wouldn't happen twice."

"What *do* you think happened?"

"Oh, I think when that ground wire came loose—and I don't really think it was vibrations, like they say, because I've seen that and this didn't look like it—the current could have jumped to the pipes during a short surge or something. Like I say, wiring is my thing, not really juice, so I don't know. Just seems likely to me."

"What do you mean it didn't look like vibrations loosened the ground wire?"

"Oh, just that when you have vibrations from pumps and motors and stuff like that, what you get is a cap that gradually unscrews over the years. The wire can still remain in contact with the post for a long time after that. I mean, it hasn't been that many years ago the local code didn't even call for caps, and we rarely had wires come loose unless they were really old. Anyway, this cap wasn't loose. The wire was away from the post all right, and it maybe vibrated out from a bad connection in the first place. But some pieces of the wire were still around the post, making me think somebody or some thing accidentally bumped that wire, either near the post or way across the other side of the basement and put enough weight or pressure on it to pull it away. I've seen that happen. I've seen kids hang on wires and pull 'em loose. I've seen women hang clothes on 'em and pull 'em loose. Anything coulda caused that."

"If there were pieces of the wire still on the post," I said, "indicating that it was pulled out somehow, how far away was the live end of the wire?"

"Not far. A few inches away."

"Then wouldn't an arc of electricity jump to the post and not to anything farther away?"

"Well, you got a point there. I never thought of that. Probably so. Like I say, I'm a wire man. Just an amateur. Listen, I'll tell you something else, though. However that juice got onto those pipes, once it was traveling along all that metal, it was going every which way."

"What are you saying?"

"Just that the guy who killed himself touching that faucet head would have killed himself no matter what he touched that was connected to those pipes. Faucets inside, metal wires attached for clotheslines, you name it."

I wasn't sure how important that last bit of news was, but I knew this guy was too uninformed and terribly naive to think nothing suspicious had gone on in that house. Significant, however, was his recollection of the way the wire had come loose. It fit our hypothesis to a T.

What I wondered as I drove back to find Margo was whether the murderer knew what he was doing. Did he simply wire that basement when he got the chance and listen for a body to fall, knowing that as soon as Rudolph touched a tap anywhere in the house he was a dead man?

If so, then as he was removing the wire and planning to reattach the ground wire, Ching and the chauffeur came in the front door. The murderer dropped the wire and headed straight out. But where? The back? A side exit? Wally would find out from Janell.

As I reached Rudolph's neighborhood again, I couldn't see Margo. I waited in the car, hoping maybe she could see me from inside somewhere. I began getting anxious after about twenty-five minutes, got out of the car, and began a casual search.

Chapter Eleven

I paced up and down the lakeside drive trying to determine whether Margo was just sitting and chatting in someone's living room or was onto something I should know about. Red flashing lights made me spin around in the street. Squad cars were pulling up to the Rudolph cottage.

I ran back to find several Wisconsin State troopers roping off the entire house and yard. "What's goin' on?" I asked one.

"Who's askin'?"

"I'm just an interested party, that's all."

"You wouldn't be Philip Spence, wouldya?"

My heart nearly stopped. How could he know that? Had something happened to Margo? I nodded.

"Do you have any form of identification?"

I produced my business card.

"Now tell me what EH stands for on this card, and I'll tell you what's goin' on."

"Earl Haymeyer," I said weakly.

"You win the prize, kid. Your boss, a former Chicago cop with a funny name—"

"Festschrift."

"Whatever. He came up with evidence that this death here last Sunday might not have been accidental. An' he also had evidence that the local sheriff's office may have glossed over the investigation. So he went to Haymeyer, head of your state law enforcement group, right?"

I nodded.

"And he got in touch with us. We'll make sure the place gets a good once over. We were told you and your wife—" he looked at a slip of paper "—Margo were up here."

"We are, but right now I can't seem to locate her."

Just then she came jogging up, out of breath.

"Philip! I got some good stuff," she said. "What's going on here?"

I told her.

The trooper added, "Apparently we're supposed to locate a side entrance to the cottage, similar to a storm cellar. Slanted doors that start in the basement, then lead to an incline of just soil and then outside. We'll be taking shoe prints if we can find any, and you can run them back to Chicago tonight, if you would."

"Happy to," I said, realizing that Wally had had good luck with Janell and wondering what else he had learned.

"What'd you get, Mar?"

"A woman right next door—which is where I should have started—had a perfect view of the back yard. She's at an angle where she can see both the back and this side. She saw Rudolph on the deck reading a paper he had brought out from the cottage. The next time she glanced out, the paper was beginning to blow off the picnic table and Rudolph was lying near the water spigot. She said the limo was parked out front, and Ching and the driver were coming in the front door."

"Where's that storm cellar type exit?" I asked the cop.

"They should have found it by now," he said. "Come on."

We walked around to the side of the cottage opposite where the woman saw Rudolph. Technicians were already crouched in the side exit, applying a synthetic mixture to the ground. Daylight was fast fading, and they worked in the shadows of high beam lights. Neighbors were gathering, but the troopers held them back. The cop swore. "This shoulda been done last Sunday."

"Did you have jurisdiction here?"

"We have it anywhere we want if the state says so. By the way, you're supposed to call your boss."

"Before you call, Philip," Margo said, "I need to tell you that a few people down the way, a couple of hundred yards south, saw a black sports car—they said it looked expensive and not like an American car—parked near the woods on the right side of the road shortly after noon on Sunday. One said it wasn't there until after one; the other wasn't sure.

"One woman was sure that whoever returned to it and drove away had to enter from the passenger's side near the woods, because she happened to be looking out and didn't see anyone get in. Suddenly the car took off."

"No license numbers or makes or models, I s'pose."

"Nope."

"I'll tell Wally."

In truth, Wally had more news for me than I did for him. "The floor plan of the cottage Janell drew for me was great," he said. "It proves one thing for sure. Whoever pulled this job had been there before."

"Are you leaning toward the son?" I asked.

"No, not at all. I talked to him and a few of his associates. The black foreign sports car is a convenient coincidence for the murderer, but Keith met his father up here on Friday night and left Saturday night. He has good witnesses and a solid alibi. You'll be interested to know what he and his father discussed last Saturday, though."

"What's that?"

"His father offered him the presidency of Plas-Techs Limited."

"You've got to be kidding. After the offer he made to Vincent Moorehouse? Was Rudolph more of a scoundrel than we thought?"

"I was getting a pretty fair impression of him as an honest businessman from Moorehouse," Wally said. "Weren't you?"

"Yeah. I can't say much for his personal life, but he seemed like a straight shooter with Vincent."

"Well, I think our impression of him—or I should say Moorehouse's impression of him—is the accurate one."

"Then how do you account for this double dealing, Wally? Offering his son a job he had assured Moorehouse was secure."

"Guess who the snake in the grass is, Philip?"

"I couldn't begin to wonder."

"One Zachary Hayes."

"What now?"

"Keith Rudolph, who seems a pretty nice guy, all things considered, tells me that his father learned that Moorehouse was trying desperately to find a white knight, and short of that, he was going to stay on and sabotage the company."

"And, of course, Adrian told Keith where he got that juicy falsehood."

"Of course. From his faithful, personal lawyer."

"Wally, what is Hayes up to?"

"What was your line, Philip—'I couldn't begin to wonder'? I guess he's so impressed with power and so greedy that if he can't get to someone one way, he'll get to them another. He's got his irons in so many fires, he's gonna burn his fingers off."

"Is he our man, Wally?"

"I don't know. I've got to find out what kind of car he drives, see if he can establish an alibi for Sunday morning, and see if any shoe prints they can pull from that exit match his."

"What do you make of this newspaper thing?" I asked.

"You mean the fact that there was a Sunday morning paper in the yard and no one knew where it came from? I think it could be one of our strongest clues, Philip. Unless you find someone who knows where Rudolph got it, we have to assume that the murderer brought it from Chicago. That places our murderer in Chicago as late as Saturday night, and in Wisconsin in time to pull the job. Apparently whoever it was was trying to implicate the chauffeur. It had to be someone who knew that the chauffeur customarily brought the Sunday morning *Trib*."

"Did you talk to the chauffeur?"

"Yeah. He was pretty defensive. Claims he shouldn't even be suspected because he found the body, and besides, he liked Rudolph. Which is probably true. He swears he brought him up to the cottage alone and that he knew the son was driving up on his own for a meeting. As far as he knows, there were no plans for the old man to have any other visitors."

"Who else would have had information like that?" I said.

"I don't know. Why?"

"Seems whoever did this would have to know things like that, Wally. They had to know he was alone in the cottage, had to know that a newspaper might implicate the chauffeur, had to know how to get in or know him well enough to be let in without a great deal of suspicion, and had to know a fast way out in an emergency."

"True enough. That seems to point to his wife, doesn't it? Or at least one of the inner circle. I'll try to establish alibis for everybody. You and Margo see if there's a straight, secluded shot from the storm cellar exit to where the people saw the black car. I'll see you at eight tomorrow, and you'll have the footprint casts, right?"

"Right. Good night, Wally."

Exhausted as we were, Margo and I talked all the way back to Chicago. "You know what's bizarre?" I said. "Stretch and I took almost the same route through the back yard that the murderer must have taken. What do you make of their finding similar heel print portions around near the front of the cottage?"

"I've been thinking about that," Margo said. "You

know, whoever it was probably sneaked in the house, otherwise why come and go the back way? Rudolph probably would have been suspicious of someone knocking on the backdoor or ringing the bell. Wanna hear my theory?"

" 'Course."

"I think the murderer parked at the side of the road and came through the woody area past the birdhouse. He went around to the front, rang the doorbell, and left the newspaper, then immediately went back around the house and quietly entered the backdoor."

"So what's Rudolph supposed to make of his first-ever delivered *Tribune?*"

"He could think it's a special promotion, or even a prank by his chauffeur. When he sees no one, he's glad to have the paper anyway, and given that he's all packed and ready to go, he heads out to the deck in the back to start reading. As the sun gets high in the sky, he goes to turn on the sprinkler system, as usual, assuming that Ching or his assistant who will arrive later will turn it off."

"You're implying that the perpetrator could have wired the pipes and waited some time before Rudolph killed himself. Why not leave immediately?"

"The murderer might have been able to go out the front and around the same way undetected, but when he gets to the back yard, he's in Rudolph's direct line of sight. He had to wait until Rudolph went inside or touched the spigot outside."

"Then did the murderer immediately remove the wire, or could he have come back or waited or anything?"

"No. There were no burns on the body that would have been caused by continued direct contact with the current. Once Rudolph got enough juice to stop his heart, the murderer pulled the wire down and then dropped it and headed for the side exit when he heard footsteps upstairs. The first plan might have been to escape through the back."

"I'm impressed, sweetheart. Either you've become the consummate detective, or you've got a great imagination. Recreating what might have happened from all the seemingly unrelated pieces of evidence is not one of my gifts."

"Don't worry about it," she said with a wink. "Stay close and I'll cover for you."

"Margo, did those prints look like running shoes to you?"

"Yes, and small ones too, but there isn't much to go on there. Just portions. The state trooper technician said it appeared to him someone was either very careful not to place his foot flat at any point or was in a terrible hurry."

"I'll vote for the latter, based on your hypothesis," I said.

"Philip."

"Hm?"

"Do you think Mrs. Rudolph paid to have this done?"

"Have you ruled *her* out?"

"You mean as the murderer? I think so," she said.

"Why?"

"She's bigger than most of the men in Rudolph's sphere of influence. Could she have pulled this off? Would she have had to sneak in and out? Couldn't

109

she have just done it, then screamed when she 'found' the body and played innocent?"

"I suppose."

"But how about her having arranged it?"

"Could be. Maybe Manfred the Wonder Lawyer was in on it."

"Motive?"

"Getting next to her. More power, more money."

"But he wouldn't have been agile enough to do it himself," Margo said.

"Or dumb enough."

When we had finally discussed all the possibilities, Margo asked how or what I was feeling about Janell by now.

"I couldn't be more disappointed, I guess. I feel like I've failed her, but—"

"It wasn't your fault, Philip. What else could you have done?"

"—yeah, I guess."

"Is there anything I can do for her besides pray for her?" Margo said.

"I don't know. You want to try to talk to her? You can't let on that you overheard our conversation the other night."

"I know. But it's not like we have more in common because we're women or anything like that. She's in a different world, Philip. I know that's no excuse, and I shouldn't shrink from speaking up about important things just because I don't measure up to someone, but—"

"Don't measure up? *She's* the one who doesn't measure up!"

"You know what I mean. She has to see me as

110

some weak, submissive, goody two-shoes. Anyway, is there anything I could tell her that she doesn't already know? She's heard the whole story, the gospel, your witness. She's apparently sat under good preaching, ran with some solid Christian kids. I believe she's made her choice, Philip, and God wasn't it."

"I hate to give up on her, though."

"Me too. But I wonder if it's to the point now where words mean much less than actions. We need to accept her and love her as she is, and show her that we're happy with each other and in Christ, without every material possession available in the universe."

"I used to think that was the only way to witness," I said, "to let people know what Christ could do in their lives. But I wonder how many people have actually been *lived* into the kingdom."

"I know what you mean, Philip. At some point they have to see themselves for what they are and see the alternative, but they have to know what the source of that alternative is. It's easy for a person to see that if he becomes honest and upright and straight overnight, he will have a new bunch of friends and will be perceived differently. And he'll even feel better about himself. But that doesn't mean he's really become a Christian and has taken care of the core problem."

"But see, Janell knows all about the alternative. She doesn't really have to ask, does she? I mean, do you think she'll ever come to me and tell me she realizes she's been wrong?"

"Only when she hits bottom, Philip. Rock bottom."

Chapter Twelve

By nine o'clock the next morning, Wally had a friend freelancing a lab check on the shoe prints provided the Wisconsin State Police. Margo and I had been filled in on Wally's productive previous afternoon and evening—and vice versa—and Wally had received two bits of news, one disappointing, the other shocking.

First, his attempt to interview Mrs. Rudolph failed. He had called Mid-America and asked to speak with her, but was denied. He was able to determine that she was indeed in the office the day after her husband's funeral, as she had been every day since his death. However, when he requested an interview in the interest of putting to rest certain questions of suspicion surrounding the incident, he was given to Manfred Towns, the corporate counsel.

"What is it exactly that you want to discuss with Mrs. Rudolph?" he asked Wally, who had the conversation punched up on the speaker phone so Margo and I could hear.

"It's a personal matter, a private investigation."

"I serve as her counsel and would be in on any such interview anyway, Mr., ah—"

"Festschrift. Walvoord Festschrift of the EH Detective Agency."

"I'm afraid, Mr. Fest— Mr. Festive— sir, that Mrs. Rudolph will not be psychologically able to bear up under any discussion of her husband's passing until next week."

"Oh, I see. She's able to carry on *his* business in *his* chair behind *his* desk in *his* office, but she can't stand the thought of talking about *him*, is that it?"

"Excuse me, sir, but that attitude—"

"My attitude is that if I were Mrs. Rudolph I would want to be aware of some very enlightening evidence and information that's come to light regarding my husband's death."

"I'm afraid that will be impossible until at least Saturday."

"Oh, we've moved from next week to Saturday? Is there any more flexibility in that schedule? Can we squeeze into Friday? Perhaps after the takeover?"

"I beg your pardon."

"If you're not protecting her until after the takeover of PlasTechs Limited, then let's make it today, shall we?"

"Drop dead, Mr. whatever-your-name-is," and Towns hung up.

Wally slammed the phone down. Earlier, he had been quite taken with Margo's idea of how the murder had taken place. Now he wanted us to look at the party list from the cottage bash Mid-America threw for a few close friends on Friday, the thirteenth of August.

"The chauffeur was there," he said. "Ching and his assistant. Towns. Mrs. Rudolph. Does that surprise you? It surprised me, but anything for looks, I guess. Hayes and his mousy wife. Keith Rudolph and his wife. Janell. And here's one that surprises me—Bee-Bee and his mother. Divorce and all that is one thing, but havin' to see your ex and your former in-laws all the time, I don't get it. I asked Janell about it. She says the Barnards and the Rudolphs go back a long way. Old money."

The phone rang. The speaker system was still on. "EH Detective Agency, Festschrift."

"Hi, Mr. Festschrift, this is Vincent Moorehouse with PlasTechs."

"Vincent, how are you, my friend?"

"Not too well, I'm afraid."

"Oh?"

"I just got a call from Zachary Hayes."

"Don't tell me he's going to file suit against you for being mean to him?" And Wally laughed.

"Frankly, I wish it were that simple, Mr. Festschrift. He asked me if I had changed my mind. I'm afraid I was rather graphic in emphasizing the negative."

"I see."

"He said it was too bad because he had been successful in arranging for another corporation, an investment company, to rescue us from Mid-America. Well, I didn't know what to say. He was such a scoundrel I didn't want to have anything to do with him. I mean, you were right; I had made a serious error in listening to him in the first place. I was just silent."

"What did he say?"

"Nothing for a while. He was enjoying having me over a barrel, especially knowing how badly I wanted to keep the company from Mrs. Rudolph. I was

114

almost ready to listen to him, but the way he asked the next question made me blow my top. He said, 'So maybe now you're ready to release my fees for services rendered and come to terms with me to represent you to the interested party. You've got about an hour to decide.' "

"What did he mean by that?"

"Well, if anyone is going to bail us out now, they have to get on it right away. At a minute after midnight tonight, we become a wholly owned subsidiary of Mid-American Maritime Properties. I don't want to be one of their properties, and Hayes knows that."

"So what did you say?"

"I was so irritated by his tone that I told him off and told him I'd die before he'd represent me to anyone. I told him that whoever was interested in PlasTechs Limited knew where to find me. He asked if I was sure and if that was my final decision. I said yes."

"Good for you."

"That's not all. He called not five minutes later, as if we had never met, let alone had a falling out. He identified himself as Zachary Hayes, an attorney representing an investor who was bidding ten dollars per share higher than Mid-America for our company. I didn't know what to think. I got a little foul and also asked Zack what in the world he thought he was trying to pull. He wouldn't be incited. He just continued calmly and said that since he was representing a company that had good faith, they had asked him to inform me of their tender and to express that they hoped I would agree that it was a

115

move in the best interests of both companies, under the circumstances."

"So when Zack couldn't get a piece of the selling action from your end, he immediately went for a cut of the buying end."

"Which is more lucrative anyway, Mr. Festschrift. And he had to have been involved with them for some time. These things don't happen in a matter of days."

"So what do you know about the company who's buying you out?"

"I know they've got a lot of money. They're committing capital to the business above and beyond the sale price. It really doesn't look half bad, though I'm not entirely happy with what sounds like an inexperienced management setup. They haven't really managed a company before."

"Who is it, anyway?" Wally asked.

We heard Moorehouse rattle a few papers. "The firm name is Barnell Investments. They will not have need of my services except as a six-month consultant, because one of their people is going to be president. A gal, the part owner. Name's, uh, Barnard. Janell Barnard. Don't know if she's the *Bar* half of the company or the *nell*, ya know?"

"Thanks for calling, Vincent. And for letting me know. I feel bad for you and your company, but I appreciate your keeping me informed."

"Thank you, Mr. Festschrift. Let's keep in touch, huh?"

"If I live to be a hundred . . ." Wally said. He looked at each of us. "I couldn't do it. I couldn't tell him he'd been bought out by our client. I just

116

couldn't. I'd better tell him before he finds out for himself or he'll think everybody in town is two-faced."

"Wally, where do you think Janell is getting the millions necessary for that purchase?"

"From BeeBee, who else? It was probably part of their marriage and divorce contract. I mean, they just can't stand each other; that doesn't mean they can't get rich together. I wonder when we'll hear from Janell."

Wally knew she'd be calling any time, so he started filling us in on the background material he had been able to obtain on the party guests of Adrian Rudolph. We gathered around one of the desks in the outer office, where he laid out his handwritten notes on yellow legal-size sheets.

Besides trying to confirm alibis, he had gone to the trouble of calling places of employment, schools, and even references where possible. "Not too many of them have any areas of concern as far as behavior goes, as you can see," he said. "The Hayeses have interesting similarities in their backgrounds. Both went to Illinois Institute of Technology. He was at the Kent law school part. Both were troublemakers in the late sixties, but nothing serious.

"Manfred Towns was fired from two jobs before landing his position with Mid-America two decades ago. Has a few underworld connections; made me wonder if he could have arranged this death, but it certainly wasn't gangland style."

"What did Hayes's wife, uh—"

"Theresa."

"Right, what did she study at I.I.T?"

"Not much. She started on the technical side in computer science and some basic required science courses, but she quit after they got married, somewhere in the middle of her second year. She was doing poorly anyway. Got a job at T and W in Lincolnwood and put him through school. She was an engineer of some sort, so something of what she learned must have stuck with her."

"What about BeeBee?"

"Typical Ivy League wimp. Now Margo, I see that look on your face. No, I'm not sayin' that everyone in the Ivy League is a wimp; in fact, most of 'em aren't. But you mix the two and you've got a real winner, like this guy. Pampered and protected, big donor to the school—the whole wad."

The phone rang. "Bet that's Janell," Wally said.

"EH, this is Margo Spence . . . . Oh, yes, sir. Just one moment. Wally? It's your friend at the lab!"

"Thanks, Mar. Punch up the speaker. Hey, Jumbo, thanks for callin'. Fast work. Wha'dya got for me?"

"Something good, I hope. You didn't give me much to work with, but it was better than some. What you've got here is a man's running shoe, very exclusive, very expensive, a size seven. It matches a brand called Luge, and the particular style is their top of the line suede. I know you didn't want me to do any of your work, but we got lucky. One of the guys here got his direct from a factory outlet. I called 'em and asked where they got 'em. They put me onto the midwest distributor for a Korean company, and they told me they only distribute to the factory outlet and one wholesaler in this area, North Shore Fitness Products. Wally, you're only gonna buy these shoes in about eight sporting goods stores and a couple of exclusive department stores. Same place you get three hundred dollar briefcases."

"Wrong, Jumbo. Where *you* buy three hundred dollar brief cases. You should see what they can do with vinyl these days! Ha! So, what else?"

"What else? If I knew exactly what kind of soil these prints came from, I could tell you how heavy this person is. We're talking light though, regardless. That's about it, Wally, unless you want me to start calling the shoe places and asking them who they sell those to. They're ninety-five dollar shoes, Wal."

"Jumbo, you're a dream. Give the list to my man here, and send me a bill, hear?"

"I heard that."

Wally handed me the phone, and I made a list of the ten stores and the factory outlet where a wealthy North Shore type could buy his ninety-five dollar running shoes. I was then to try to match the locations with the addresses of the party guests. While I was studying that, Janell called.

"Yes," Wally said, faking ebullience, "I can't tell you how surprised I was to hear the news. Are congratulations in order?"

"Sure, thank you so much. I'm so excited I can hardly stand it."

"You're going to be the new president, are you?"

"Yes, isn't that exciting?"

"Well, my, my. I met the current president today, and he'll be quite an act to follow. But I'm sure that doesn't faze you."

"No, it doesn't, Wally. I'm looking forward to it.

119

Of course, we've got twenty days to wait to see if Mid-America or anyone else wants to up the ante. I sure hope no one does, and don't tell anyone, but we're prepared to go much higher. I'm so pleased."

"For you or because Mid-America was thwarted."

"Good question, Wally, and hard to decide. How's the search going, by the way?"

"It was murder, Janell."

Silence. Finally she spoke. "I was right then?"

"Yes, ma'am, you sure were. I have enough evidence to prove it was murder, but I'm afraid it wouldn't stop the merger because the murderer is neither an employee of Mid-America nor of PlasTechs."

"Oh? You know who it is?"

"I'll know by the time you get here, Janell. You owe me some money. I know we didn't stop the merger; you did. But the deal was that we tell you it was murder and be able to prove it by midnight."

"I'm dying to know."

"I'll bet you are."

"You want me to come there?"

"Exactly."

"Now?"

"As soon as you can round up your friends."

"My friends?"

"The ones who are closest to you right now. The ones who are in on this acquisition with you. Tell them I'm so intrigued by your aggressiveness that I want to help you celebrate. But don't tell any of them where they're going."

"What if they can't come, Wally? I believe Bernard's mother is under the weather."

"If you get them all here but Mrs. Barnard, that will suffice."

"I'll try, Wally," she said, slowly, puzzled.

"Don't try, Janell. Do it. Show me what kind of a corporate president you are. Make a directive. Be firm. Find out who wants to be seen with the boss and who doesn't, who wants to make points and who doesn't."

"I'm not Bernard's boss. We're partners in this."

"Yeah, like you were partners in your marriage. You ran him then, you engineered the contract and the divorce, and you've run him ever since. He'll do what you say because he knows you mean money to him. Bring him, Janell. He'll enjoy the celebration."

"What time, Wally?"

"As soon as you can round them up. I'll have the champagne ready, and soft drinks for my teetotaling employees."

"Wally?"

"Yes, dear."

"You're not going to tell me who the murderer is in front of everyone, are you?"

"Maybe you'll tell *me*. I'll see you soon, Janell. Bye."

Wally turned to Margo. "Call Jumbo and ask him how fast he can make a mock-up of the entire sole of the shoe we found. I'll pick it up while I'm out."

"I've got one other quick call to make, too," she said, removing one of his yellow sheets from the desk. "If you don't mind my playing a hunch."

"Not at all. And Philip, call those stores. Tell them you need to get in touch with someone who bought those model shoes. You need a reference or a recommendation, and they have to be from one of the towns on your list. When I get back with the champagne, we've got to have all our ducks in a row."

"You know who we're looking for, Wally?" I said.

"Let's just say I've got it narrowed down and that I won't be terribly surprised. Neither will you."

Chapter Thirteen

I had the feeling Wally was doing more than buying champagne and soft drinks. He was gone quite a while, and when he returned, I had a message for him.

"Janell called," I said. "She's quite upset. She says Mid-America put a stop payment notice on her severance check, which she just got around to trying to cash today. They're filing suit against her, claiming she had an unfair advantage in this new bid because of having worked with Mid-America."

Wally got a kick out of that, but he was concerned about what it meant for his party.

"Have no fear," I said. "She's returned the invitation. She wants us to join her for dinner at her place tonight."

"Same guest list?"

"I don't know. She left a number."

Wally buried the receiver in the crook of his neck and punched out her number while idly digging into a plain brown wrapper and producing a plaster mold of the shoe print found at the Rudolph cottage. He toyed with it as he chatted with her.

"Yeah, Janell, can I still bring the champagne? Good! Listen, who all's gonna be there? I like big parties! Your partner, uh-huh. His mother? Oh, past her bedtime, huh? Your lawyer and his wife? Good, uh-huh. And the three of us, are you sure? We'd love to! Anyone else? Well, you could ask him, but I think Mr. Moorehouse and his wife would not be predisposed to coming, no. Will you do me a favor, Janell? I'd like to come a little later than the others; I should say all three of us would arrive—say—ten minutes after the others. That's all right? Well, here's the favor. I'd like you to not tell the others who else is expected. Right, just tell 'em you have three surprise guests, OK? Thanks, Janell. Sorry to hear about your check from Mid-America. You think it's because of the higher bid? You don't? He is? Yes, you forgot to include him and his wife when you rattled the list off there. No kidding? No, I didn't expect that. He'll serve on your staff there at PlasTechs as what, an executive? Executive vice-president and general manager. I see. Well, that should put Mr. Moorehouse's mind at ease. Well, no, he was just curious about the management experience and all. So that makes how many tonight? Nine? I'll be the only one without a date! I wish BeeBee's mother could make it. Ha! But you think that he's the reason they're being sticky on your check? They owe you how much? Forty-three five, but that includes the extra thousand you didn't understand. Maybe it was your partial paycheck before the severance, you think? No? You'd give them the thousand to take the forty-two five, wouldn't you? Yeah, I would too. Listen, that isn't the money you were going to pay me out of, was it? It was? Oh, no, that will be fine. No, I'll accept any check drawn on BeeBee's account. No problem. It could even wait a week, if you wish. I'll see you at about six-fifteen then, dear. And thanks again."

"So who are the mystery guests?" Margo asked when Wally hung up.

"Wait and see," he said. "How'd your hunch work out?"

"I'm not quite sure yet. I have to call back. Or maybe I don't. Maybe one of you could tell me. What's a finishing supervisor?"

"Depends," I said. "You mean like in a factory?"

"I guess, yeah."

"The person in charge of seeing that the product, whatever it is, is finished."

"Meaning what?"

"Depends on the product," I said. "Might mean that the final screws are in and it's painted, polished, or sanded. I hope after all this expert input, you're gonna tell us what you're after."

"Maybe. Maybe not. How important would it be for a finishing supervisor to know what goes into the product before it gets to the finishing stage?"

"Again, it depends on the product," Wally said. "But if it has to be painted or coated or something, the finishing supervisor should know as much as the designer, because the chemicals he chooses could be that important."

Margo nodded slowly. "One more call," she said. "Then I might have something for you."

"And what are *you* up to, cowboy?" Wally asked me.

"I've got a list of the stores who carry Luge shoes and the people from your list who have accounts at one of them. I'm afraid they almost all do, Wally. We should have expected that wealthy people would have accounts in exclusive shops. I can't get any of the stores to tell me whether those people bought the running shoes in a size seven for men, so I'm on another project right now."

"Which is?"

"I'm checking with the *Tribune* to see how many of those people subscribe."

"It's still basically a Republican paper," Wally said, laughing. "These bourgeois types will all be subscribers!"

He was right, of course. Late in the afternoon, when I finally presented him my lists of suspects and their accounts and newspaper subscriptions, I wasn't sure I was giving him much.

Margo, on the other hand, rather smugly folded a single sheet of paper and marched it over to him. He unfolded it, read it, smiled, and deposited it in his shirt pocket. Wally gathered up the loose yellow sheets on the desk, put them together with his dog-eared note pad, and carried them into his office.

"I'm gonna be studying and memorizing for a while," he said. "And then I'm goin' down the hall and dress for dinner. I imagine we'll be on the humble end of the spectrum tonight, so if you want to go home and get gussied up, feel free. Pick me up at quarter to six."

While we were changing at home, I chided Margo. "You're not gonna tell me what you were up to on the phone today, huh?"

"Nah. Wally wouldn't. He enjoys the big finale, the surprise ending. Anyway, you gave him information I don't know about, didn't you?"

"Yeah, but it didn't make him smile the way yours

did. I get the impression you both know who to put the finger on tonight."

"I don't, Philip. I really don't. Actually, when I put what I learned with what the crime scene and the evidence says we should be looking for, it leaves me puzzled. I do believe, though, that it all makes sense for Wally."

"That doesn't surprise me. I just wonder how he's going to pull this off tonight. I worry about Janell."

"Janell?" Margo said. "You don't suspect her, surely."

"Of course not. But I worry how she'll bear up under this. This day should be the highlight of her kind of life, but there has to be emptiness at her core. And if one of her close associates murdered a boss she cared for so much, I wonder how she'll react."

"I've been praying for her, Philip. I have to admit I envied her at first. I envied her beauty. I envied her money and her position. Her background. Her self-assurance. Her history with you."

"You had nothing to envy."

"I know that, Philip, and envy is wrong even if I did have something to envy. But when I heard her admit that she knew herself, that she could see inside herself and know who she was and what she was about and still choose that over what she knew was an alternative, I knew there was nothing you or I could say or do to change her. Only God can do that. While Wally is enjoying himself tonight, putting the spotlight on someone unaware, I'll be praying for Janell."

"You know, Margo, she could sit there and see it happen and get a hint that her world is full of wolves and foxes who would just as soon outmaneuver her and use her and devour her as to look at her, and still decide she's comfortable there."

"That's inconceivable to me, Philip, but I know why you say it. I heard her express that myself. But I won't give up on her."

I should have known what Wally meant by dressing for dinner. What he did was to dress down, on purpose. Not that he was ever a model of fashionability. But he went from a daytime outfit of brown wing tipped shoes, brown socks, brown slacks, beige shirt, and dark brown tie to a dinner ensemble of black, thick-soled shoes, white socks, blue slacks, yellow shirt, no tie, and green and white checked coat. He was intentionally separating himself from his audience, even from us. When I first met Wally, I thought he dressed carelessly. I've since learned that little if anything Wally ever does is without reason.

He was strangely silent on the drive downtown to Janell's apartment. He brought no notes, and I got the impression he was rehearsing in his mind all the facts he thought he needed for the encounter. As we pulled into the underground parking garage at Janell's building, he suddenly spoke. "Just wait till you see the expression on Hayes's face when he finds out we're the mystery guests!"

The doorman was the first surprised face we had to get past. He checked our names off a pre-approved list, but couldn't stop himself from looking Wally up and down and saying, "*You're* Mr. Festschrift?"

And as if he had not caught the edge to the man's

voice, Wally loudly responded with a hearty handshake, and "That's right, sir, and your name?"

"Charles," the man said, shaken.

"Well, good to see *you* tonight, Charles!"

When Janell opened the door, the rest of her guests were standing and sitting, munching. I saw a tall, slender couple in their mid-thirties who were dark and dramatically handsome who could have passed for brother and sister. I knew immediately that this must be the man Janell had tabbed as executive vice president and general manager of PlasTechs Limited. Wally approached and said, "Keith and Mrs. Rudolph, how are you? Good to see you again."

So, Keith was still on the outs with his mother. Working for the enemy would really nail the lid in that coffin.

Meanwhile, little Zachary Hayes, dressed to kill, left his blond, curly-haired, pointy-faced wife sitting on the sofa (she appeared every bit as large as he was) as he bounced to his feet and dragged Janell into the kitchen, where caterers were busy. I maneuvered close enough to hear him asking what we were doing there and her telling him that we had represented her in investigating Rudolph's death.

"I don't think I can stay," I heard as I drew closer. "The man humiliated and embarrassed me and made slanderous allegations when I was negotiating with PlasTechs the other day."

"Whatever happened?" Janell asked, incredulous.

"I was there to tender your offer when that fat man with the weird name accused me of playing both ends against the middle and—"

Wally approached and pecked Janell on the cheek

and threw an arm around Hayes's shoulder. "Zack!" he bellowed. "We can't go on meeting like this! Ha! Ha! Janell, it smells great! When are the eats on?"

When Hayes moved away, Wally squinted at me and I knew what he wanted. He was saying, "Don't let him leave."

"Mr. Hayes," I called with great deference, as he reached his wife and leaned down to help her off the sofa. She wasn't about to move and looked at him like he'd lost his mind. To escape embarrassment, he turned to me.

"Yes, yes, what?"

"I understand you graduated from Kent at I.I.T."

"That's right. What about it?"

"Did you happen to know Noel Krey?"

"Who?"

"Noel Krey."

"When did he attend Kent?"

"He didn't. He majored in photography at I.I.T. Graduated in seventy-one, I think."

"Then I wouldn't know him."

"Good school," I said.

"Right."

"You like it?"

"Sure. It's served me well, having gone there. No complaints."

By now his wife was deep into a conversation with Mrs. Rudolph, and Hayes's urgency to escape had been lost. I was dragged away to meet Bernard Barnard and realized quickly what Wally had meant about his wimpy handshake.

He was a short, prissy man dressed in a lot of burgundy. There was taste and expense in the clothes, but wimp in the manner. Just my luck, Janell called us to her long dining room table and put me in the middle on one side with Margo on my left and Bee-Bee on my right.

Janell sat at one end, to BeeBee's right, and she put Wally at the other end, to Margo's left. On the other side of the table, left to right from my vantage point, were Keith and Clarice Rudolph and Zack and Theresa Hayes.

Servers brought Polynesian delicacies from the kitchen, and just when we were ready to dig in, Janell caused five double takes and nearly a whiplash for Keith when she asked if I would pray for the meal. I was so shocked I hardly had the presence to get it all out. I knew she had done it for effect, with a twinkle in her eye, to put me in my place and to see if I'd be embarrassed to be pegged for what I was.

And in a roomful of mostly strangers who were wondering what in the world we were doing there, I *was* embarrassed.

Chapter Fourteen

"I'd like to propose a toast to the hostess," Wally said, as the dishes were being cleared. "Are there any teetotalers besides my good assistants here?"

Only Janell was in as festive a mood as Wally, because the rest of us either knew all too well what was coming, or were afraid to guess. The Rudolphs had been very quiet throughout the meal, and so had Zack Hayes. His wife and Janell had dominated the conversation when Wally didn't have the floor.

I wasn't sure yet if BeeBee had a voice box or not.

After everyone but Margo and I had sipped champagne, Wally stared straight down the table at Janell. "I think I'd like to bring you up to date on the investigation," he said. "Mind if I do it right here?"

"What investigation?" BeeBee said, finally speaking up. "You said you were involved in some sort of a business relationship with Janell."

"That's right. May I tell him, Janell?"

"Well, I'd really rather—"

"Yes, let him tell us, Janell," Theresa Hayes said. "Why the big mystery?"

The Rudolphs appeared amused, assuming we were part of an elaborate practical joke Janell was pulling.

Wally still hesitated, waiting for Janell's nod.

"C'mon, Janell!" Theresa begged.

"Yeah, c'mon," Keith added. "Let us in on it."

Janell nodded reluctantly to Wally, fear written on her face.

"This may not be too terribly pleasant," Wally said. "Especially to you, Mr. Rudolph, because it concerns the murder of your father."

Keith had been leaning forward, his chin resting on one fist. Now his hand dropped slowly to the table, and he looked down at Janell. It appeared he might stand, but he didn't. He looked to his wife who was suddenly pale.

"I asked him to investigate it for me," Janell explained breathlessly. "You know how much I admired your father, Keith, and I just couldn't rest until I knew what happened there."

"It didn't take us long to determine that someone deliberately caused that death, Mr. Rudolph. It was someone who knew that cottage and that area and who knew your father's habits and the habits of his staff. It was someone close to your father, or close to someone who knew a lot about him."

Zack Hayes sat with his lips pressed tight, alternately glaring at Wally and staring at the tablecloth. His wife's chest heaved as if she were hyperventilating. BeeBee looked lost.

Wally described the murder sequence as Margo had recreated it after examining all the findings. Keith Rudolph's breath began to come in short bursts through his nose as he fought to keep control of his emotions. His dark eyes flashed, and his wife took his hand in hers.

"You can see why we're led to believe that this job

133

was handled by someone who knew a little about electricity. It was also done by someone whose foot would fit an expensive running shoe about this size." He pulled out the cast and slapped it on the table, sending slivers of plaster sliding toward the left side. Keith jumped.

"You see," Wally said gently, "these shoes, these Luge running shoes, are the shoes to have. There are only so many places you can buy them, and almost everyone at this table has accounts at those stores. Now what we need to know is whether the person who had the opportunity also had the means and the motive. Mrs. Rudolph, you might have had a motive."

Her eyes grew large and her mouth fell open. "I, but I, I couldn't, I wouldn't do something like that! I never even considered, why, especially after their last meeting. If you knew about their last meeting, you'd know neither of us had a motive!"

Wally raised the fingers of his left hand to quiet her. "I really don't believe, Mrs. Rudolph, that this shoe would fit you. I'm not going to ask your size, but your height demands a larger foot than a size seven men's shoe."

She swallowed and her hands shook. "I'm five-ten," she said, "and I wear a nine woman's shoe. I really don't know how that corresponds with a man's shoe. I should tell you, I've never jogged. I have deck shoes."

"Mr. Festschrift," Keith said, "even if my wife had a motive at one time, she doesn't have the knowledge required to do what you said was done. The black car someone saw in that neighborhood wasn't ours because ours was at home. We were at home. And I think you know that."

"Yes, I know that. BeeBee, what size shoe do you wear?"

He almost panicked. "I don't know," he said, his voice squeaking like an adolescent's.

"Check, man, check!" Wally said.

Bernard reached down and pulled up a patent leather and suede Gucci loafer. "It's a seven, but I don't own those jogging shoes you mentioned."

"No, and you have a fair alibi too, don't you?"

"I don't recall. Do I?"

"Yes, even though you had a motive and, who knows, maybe even some electrical knowledge, you and your mother were visiting your own father's resting place in Indiana last Sunday, were you not?"

"Yes, yes, we were," Bernard said, as if relieved to know that he couldn't have been the murderer. "And believe me, electricity scares me to death, I mean, excuse the expression."

"Anyway, Mr. Bar*nard*," Wally said, "I'm gonna bet you don't drive a black car."

"No, sir. I don't drive. When I ride, it's in either a cream Benz or a burgundy Bentley."

"How nice. Janell, I want to tell you about your legal counsel. Mr. Rudolph's legal counsel. And until yesterday, Vincent Moorehouse's legal counsel."

"Oh, he wasn't representing Mr. Moore—" Janell began, but Hayes interrupted.

"I'm warning you, Freshkeet or whatever your name is. You start this again about—"

"You're warning *me*, Zack?" Festschrift said.

"What're you gonna do, electrocute me? You don't threaten me, Zack. Let me advise the adviser and counsel the counselor. You can get up and run outa here and make faces at me the way you did in Moorehouse's office the other day, but I'm gonna say what I want to say about you whether you're here or not. And if you run out that door, you're gonna run right into the arms of the Wisconsin State Police who are in the hall with a warrant."

"Oh, Mr. Festschrift," Keith said, "I don't believe you understand the unique relationship that Zack has had with my father for many years."

"Let *me* just tell *you* about it, all right?" Wally said. "Zack wanted in on the merger. Janell, you saw that in his own handwriting."

"Yes, but—"

"But it was too late and maybe next time, right, Zack? So Zack runs over to PlasTechs and tries to represent them on the selling end, even to the point of pretending to find them an angel. But, wonder of wonders, the best angel of all comes along once Mr. Rudolph dies. All of a sudden, everybody's favorite lawyer is representing everyone in town. When the PlasTechs deal blows up in his face, he represents BeeBee's money and Janell's interest, but believe me if there had been a way for him to take fees on both sides, he would have done it. How would you do that, Zack, with a pen name?"

"You're not going to get away with accusing me of murder, fat man," Zack said. "I had a racquetball date Sunday morning. And I don't drive a black car. I drive a silver BMW, and everybody knows it. Yeah, I've got Luge shoes, and they're size sevens, but I lost 'em somewhere and didn't even wear 'em to the gym Sunday."

"You didn't, huh?" Wally pressed. "Where did you leave your shoes, Zack?"

"I don't know! What's that got to do with anything? I thought I had 'em in the house, in the closet, but they're lost. Anyway, I didn't have a motive! My future's better with old man Rudolph alive! I've got an alibi. I've got friends who were with me Sunday."

"I know you do. How was your Sunday *Tribune* this week, Zack? You read it before or after going to the gym?"

Zack looked puzzled. "My, um, Sunday paper didn't come this week. I had to buy one."

"You don't have a black car, right, Zack?"

Janell buried her face in her hands and began to cry.

Zack had trouble speaking. His wife stared at the table, even when many eyes were on her. "I, ah, said I don't *drive* one," Zack managed.

"But you own one, don't you, son?" Wally said.

Zack's lips trembled and he nodded miserably.

"You've got a matched set, Zack. 'Cause you're makin' it big, you got yourself a silver one and you also got a black one just like it for the little lady. Only she's not so little, is she? Fact is, she's big enough to wear your shoes, and she's been known to do it."

Theresa Hayes sat unblinking, unmoving, her jaw set. Almost imperceptibly her head began to turn back and forth as if she didn't want to hear any more.

But Wally wasn't finished. "I couldn't put it all together with your alibi, Zack," he said. "That kept getting in my way. But when my gal here checked out

137

the previous employment of people with motive and opportunity, up jumped Theresa's schooling and that good job that put you through school.

"All of a sudden, on top of the pile of a lot of people who might have wanted to see Adrian Rudolph in his grave stood a feisty little woman who was once the finishing supervisor in an electric company. And anyone who knows what kind of paint to put on a terminal box knows enough about wiring to snuff somebody.

"The opportunity? That was easy. She'd been at the parties. Her husband was gone all morning on Sunday. She had her little hot car. And she came bearing a gift. A Sunday *Tribune*. The means? Pretty crafty, and had it not been for bad timing, she'd have been even able to clear away the evidence.

"But one of the guys who scared her off by walking in the front door was also the one who cleaned up after her and unwittingly tripped her with her own little piece of wire. You weren't strong enough to snip that wire clean with the clippers, were you, honey? You had to grab it in the pliers and twist it back and forth. But oh, you knew what to do with it, once you had it cut.

"The motive? The most despicable of all. Greed and revenge. You wanted Zachary to have a piece of that merger, and the day he told you he'd been left out of it, you started plotting how to get back at Adrian Rudolph. Only you were too early. You got him before he could write his son back into his will, which would have angered his wife to the point where she would have left him. She might have taken her lawyer escort with her, leaving open a plum position for your husband in a corporation that was acquiring more properties."

Keith Rudolph stared at the ceiling, his tongue vainly trying to moisten his lips. Hoarsely, he said, "Someone help me out of here before I kill her."

His wife stood quickly and tried to help him from his chair. Wally and I went to him. As we led them into the hall, Wally whispered to the Wisconsin State trooper and a matron.

They entered and asked Mrs. Hayes to join them and asked if she wanted anyone with her. Her husband started to rise, but she shook her head. As she was led away, BeeBee put a hand on Janell's shoulder. "Are you all right?" he asked.

She nodded. "What will this mean to the merger?" she asked.

He shrugged and looked to Zack, who slowly raised his head, his eyes red. "Um, it doesn't have to, ah, hinder anything, really. It may, but I think we can forestall any serious setback."

Janell sat forward, and BeeBee leaned over and rested his elbows on the table so he could hear better. "What should we do?" Janell said.

"I'll try to get hold of Moorehouse in the morning," Zack said.

Janell and Bernard nodded, and Margo and I tried to remind ourselves that we worshiped the God of the impossible.